Empowering Employee Engagement

How to Ignite Your Team for Peak Performance

To Laddy
Shine bright daily and
be your best self with love,

Claire Cahill

Claire
Cahill x

Typeset with Garamond and Century Gothic

Edited by: Deborah Taylor, Book-Launch Your Business
PDF illustrations by: Eddie Lowden

ISBN-13: 978-1536974560

DEDICATION

To Martin, Adam, George and Henry.
The driving force in all I do.

"Claire's book is full of practical wisdom that can instantly be applied to motivate employees to perform at their peak. Her 'Do it' approach coupled with her 'Ignite' coaching programme reaffirms the incredible value and power of life coaching and how the right techniques can assist employees to boost their motivation, accelerate their performance and achieve success."

Bev James CEO of The Coaching Academy and bestselling author of *Do it! or Ditch it.*

CONTENTS

ACKNOWLEDGEMENTS

I would like to thank the following people for helping me achieve my goal of writing this book:

The Ignite team for being prepared to change.

My peers for allowing me the opportunity to play to my strengths and shine.

My line manager, Carolyn, for believing in me, empowering and encouraging me to deliver the concept.

My coaches for helping me remain focused and positive, inspiring my confidence and exploring my limiting beliefs for success.

All the fabulous women I have met on my journey to where I am now who have promoted my business to other successful business women.

All the leaders and aspiring leaders of the future who have followed my progress through social media.

My clients and followers for trusting the process and being prepared to change so they feel empowered to shine.

My friends and family who have encouraged and supported me through the challenges of writing my book.

My book coach and publisher, Deborah Taylor of Book Launch Your Business, without whose constant support, encouragement, guidance and expertise I would have quite easily given up, especially when the going got tough.

Most importantly my husband Martin, my step son Adam and my sons George and Henry for their constant support, belief and inspiration in allowing me to live my dream with passion and enthusiasm.

INTRODUCTION

Since leaving school at the age of 15, I have only ever worked for one company: a financial institution. I had always wanted to work for a bank, but in the end, I chose to work for a building society because I felt more aligned with its values and because as a business it looks after its customers first rather than its shareholders. To this, some might say, "Wow! That's dedication and loyalty", and others might say, "You're institutionalised – get a life!"

I started my career in June 1990 and my first job was as a cashier in the Worksop branch of a large UK building society. I joined as part of a Youth Trainee Scheme and when I started, I remember asking my mum why I should have to do slave labour – that's what it felt like at the time.

I stayed at the Worksop branch for five years, gradually taking on more and more responsibility, and working my way through my career development plan. I am lucky that the company I work for takes responsibility for the career development of every one of its staff. I wanted to be a Branch Manager and have my own branch, so my career plan was aimed at helping me increase my knowledge, take up opportunities and increase my skill level so I could reach my goals and fulfil my potential.

During my 26-year career, I have never been someone who has just sat around waiting for something good to come along. I've invested in my personal development, looked for new opportunities and aimed to grow both as an individual and a professional. When I started working at Worksop, I had a good relationship with the senior management team and they supported me by giving me opportunities to develop, including standing in front of a group of over 100 people to deliver corporate cascades (the method by which key messages and operational plans are filtered from top to the bottom in the business). It was an honour for me to stand in front of such a huge audience when I was just 20 years old.

I didn't realise it at the time, but this was just the start – there were even better things to come. I discovered that I enjoyed being in the limelight and felt a thrill each time I stepped out of my comfort zone. I enjoyed having sweaty palms and butterflies in my stomach because deep down I knew it was a sign that I was growing and developing.

The experience I gained during the five years at the Worksop branch gave me the courage to apply for a Customer Service Manager role at the Retford branch – and I got it! At this point, I wasn't even 21 but I was suddenly responsible for the development of four other members of staff as well as delivering challenging sales targets and customer service goals.

I built a strong working relationship with the Branch Manager at Retford and it wasn't long before we were achieving huge successes. As individuals, we were complete opposites, which made us the perfect team. We were a winning combination – and proof that opposites in business can work extremely well together. If we had both been the same in terms of personality and skills, it could have been a disaster, especially as the branch and team were so small.

At the age of 24, I got the opportunity to return to the Worksop branch on a 12-month secondment. But it meant working alongside the colleagues I had started with as a Youth Trainee. The only difference was that this time I was returning as their Branch Manager so suddenly they would be working *for* me rather than *alongside* me. I knew this was going to be a huge challenge, but I was excited.

At this stage in my career I had already achieved one of the goals I had set for myself at the age of 15, which was to be a Branch Manager and successfully run my own branch. I was now a temporary Branch Manager at

Worksop and I had 12 months to prove my worth so I could make the job permanent.

I had a great time working with my old team and, although I feared there would be some resistance from them to begin with, I had the opposite experience. The whole team seemed to trust and respect me, probably because they liked the fact that I was ambitious enough to drive them to success. In this role, I had to implement everything I had learnt from my previous roles. At the same time, I had to remember that being in the driving seat was new to me and I still had a lot to learn.

My secondment at Worksop was a success and as a result – and after winning numerous awards with the team for sales performance and outstanding customer service – it was time for me to manage a larger branch. I then went on to secure a permanent role as a Branch Manager in Rotherham. I was ecstatic! This was my moment to make my mark.

While I was successful in my new role in Rotherham, after 12 months I began to realise that something wasn't right, I no longer felt challenged. But that wasn't my only problem because I was unhappy at home too.

This made for a difficult time, but I knew there was only one person who could fix it and that was me! I was the only person who could make me happy and that was what I decided I was going to do. I ended my marriage of eight years and secured a promotion. I never do anything by halves! I've come to realise that I am an 'all or nothing' kind of girl. Others thought I was having some sort of mid-life crisis even though I was only 28. Looking back, these were two of the best decisions I ever made. (I am now happily married again with two sons and a step son and my life has never been better.)

At work, my promotion resulted in me moving into a new contact centre that was opening in Sheffield. All I had ever known was retail banking so I was very excited about being part of this new venture. I can honestly say that in the 12 years I have worked in the contact centre I have learnt more about people and performance management than I ever knew before. The other reason the contact centre was important to me was because it led me to seek out more and more personal development opportunities. Ultimately, it led me to train and work as a coach.

The more work I did on my own development, the more I realised that two of my key motivators are personal growth and a thirst for learning. I also began to discover that my strengths were with people rather than processes. I enjoyed the leadership and coaching aspects of my role more than the systems side. Working with people is what makes my heart sing and is the reason why I am so passionate about coaching.

During my time working at the building society, I have seen lots of employees, leaders and CEOs come and go, for one reason or another. However, one thing I have noticed, both while working in retail banking and at the contact centre is how important it is for a business to have happy, engaged and empowered employees.

There is constant change in all organisations and everyone adapts differently to it but it was only after I decided to follow my passion of coaching to become a qualified corporate and executive life coach that I fully understood how to help employees unlock their true potential. It is one of the reasons why I want to work with inspirational leaders in the future and share my Ignite Coaching Programme with as many businesses as possible.

In this book, I will tell the story of how nine hand-selected employees formed a special team and went on a journey of self-discovery that took them from good to great over a 12 week period.

I have organised this book in such a way that it shows how I brought together the Ignite team and how I, as the leader, had to look at myself just as closely as the team and, like them, decide whether I wanted to change or not.

Should you choose to follow the same path, I have

included details about the tools I used to help both myself and my team understand ourselves better so we could grow, change and develop. In telling you how the Ignite Team became more engaged and by sharing these coaching and management tools I hope I can help you lead your own team through a process of change towards increased engagement.

Just like myself and the Ignite team, you and your team will have to decide for yourselves whether you want to stay with or leave the business as a result of this process. What I can guarantee is that by the end you will be empowered to make your own decisions about what is best for you.

By using a coaching and leadership process to engage disillusioned employees I was able to re-ignite my team's passion and self-belief so that they could go on and achieve huge successes. So come with me on a journey of self-discovery into the magical world of Ignite and you will be able to do the same.

CHAPTER 1
BRINGING THE TEAM TOGETHER

The start of the Ignite project was as much about my own self-development and personal growth as it was about the team's. We all went on a journey together, but in order to be the Ignite team manager, I had had to go on a journey of my own.

I had been in my role for over 10 years when a new Senior Operations Manager joined the contact centre. I had been working with her for about three months and in that time, I had been through a process with her to build a relationship. It hadn't started well…

When she joined the business, I was curious to know more about her. I had questions. What was her background? Why had she been selected? What did she have to offer? Curiosity got the better of me so I looked her up on LinkedIn and read her profile. The problem is that when you look someone up on LinkedIn, you leave a footprint – so my new manager knew I'd been checking her out.

Now, I always feel good when someone looks at my profile on LinkedIn, first of all because it means someone has found me and second because it means they're sufficiently interested in me to read my profile and even connect with me. However, I believe my manager didn't take the same view. She seemed unsettled by my interest and seemed to see my curiosity as a sign of distrust. As a result, we didn't get off to the best of starts. After I checked her out, my manager went and asked other leaders in the business what they thought about me – and apparently they were keen to share their personal opinions and perceptions!

I had not had the best relationship with my previous Senior Manager so when my new manager took over, I was disengaged in my role and this showed in all my interactions. I am normally outspoken but during meetings I kept quiet because I was bored. At other times (if I set my mind to it) I was capable of being disruptive just because I wanted to get some attention. I knew I had the skills and abilities to do much more but the opportunity hadn't presented itself.

Despite the less than wonderful start, at the point when my new manager joined the company, I was ready for a change – and a challenge. I was feeling frustrated and undervalued because I knew my skills weren't being fully utilised. As a result, having someone new come into the business was exciting and I was keen to learn from her.

I wanted to build a good relationship with my new Senior Manager because I believed she was going to be a breath of fresh air. She had all the skills and abilities needed to run a successful contact centre, she had a good background and a lot of experience. I wanted to be part of her team, not least because I was excited about what I could learn from her.

As I have already mentioned, learning and self-development are key drivers for me and suddenly I had a manager I could learn from, who had a great track record and who had invested in her own personal development. She was also new to the financial services industry, so she brought experience of other organisations and industries with her. For someone like me who had only ever worked in one company this was an opportunity to establish whether or not I was institutionalised or simply loyal! There was only one problem: she didn't seem to trust me.

My manager and I had more than one open and honest conversation when we started working together and I quickly realised that if I was going to get where I wanted to go then I was going to have to change. However, there was one thing I was going to have to change quickly because it was going to be pivotal to my success – and that was my attitude! I needed to show my new boss my 'brilliant self'.

So within a few weeks, I made some important changes and it didn't take long before I started to shine. My boss started to see the seed of potential grow within me and the flower of engagement start to bloom. Soon, I was coming into work energised, enthusiastic and positive. I was forward thinking and I implemented action plans aimed at moving my team forward.

I soon noticed that the staff in my team became more engaged simply as a result of my own new-found motivation. They were inspired by me again. I saw firsthand what a difference it made when I changed my thinking and attitude. It impacted directly on my feelings and that ultimately affected my behaviour – and that of my team. From this I experienced how my own mood as the team leader affected the mood of my team. I also discovered that knowing yourself inside out is critical to success. I had direct evidence that if I changed my mood it would result in a shift in others as they followed my lead.

My feelings about myself and my role completely changed and finally I was being recognised for what I am good at: being a coach as well as an inspirational leader who thrives on change and challenge. Suddenly, I felt valued and engaged again. Even more importantly, my boss noticed my potential, too. She started to believe in me, trust me and respect me. As this was important to me and reflected my own values, I became even more motivated.

My new manager was creating a different culture and was focused on making the site a centre of excellence. To support this goal, it was suggested that the centre's managers needed to think about using employee satisfaction surveys to gauge the mood of the staff and to look at how employee enablement and engagement could be improved.

It was in a team managers' meeting that it was

suggested that someone take on a team of disengaged employees with a view to turning around their performance in the business. The theory was that by raising an employee's engagement in the business and instilling a sense of empowerment, the individual would feel a greater sense of satisfaction in their role. This in turn would raise their work satisfaction score, lead them to perform better in the business and help the company do more business.

All the team managers were asked to nominate one person from their team who they believed to be disengaged in the business. I made a radical decision to nominate an employee who had the potential to be a team manager himself but had become disengaged because he hadn't been promoted as he had expected. He had applied for the position of team manager but had been unsuccessful. He was now being disruptive and his performance was inconsistent. Under normal circumstances, he would not have gone into the new team, but because of the issue with the promotion, it was the right thing to do. Other team managers made similar decisions: the employees they chose for the Ignite Team were often absent, performed inconsistently, behaved in a disruptive way, exhibited low morale and appeared generally unhappy in their role. The next task was to decide who was going to lead this team. I volunteered without hesitation, after all, this was right up my street.

When opportunities come along I believe you have to seize the moment and grab them, even if they are scary and present challenges. That's why at this moment in the meeting, I thought. "Aha, this is a great opportunity to demonstrate my coaching skills, if I don't throw my name in the hat now I'm going to miss the chance to be involved in something new and exciting." Before I could stop myself I heard myself say, "I'll take the team". It wasn't clear at this stage what I had volunteered for, but I knew it felt right. Sometimes you can't sit around and wait for everything to be in place, you have to take a leap of faith and know that the net will catch you, and this is exactly what I did when I volunteered to take on the new team.

As a qualified coach, I knew had the skills, capability and passion to take the group of nine people on a journey of self-discovery to re-engage them back into the business. When I discovered that others had the same confidence in me, I didn't look back. I realised that this was my golden opportunity to shine. The icing on the cake came when my manager endorsed me and gave me a little wink of encouragement – then it was all systems go!

Having gained the trust of the key stakeholders in running my 12-week Ignite Programme, it was important to me (and the management team as a whole) that I had a plan that was structured, bespoke and flexible. I was going to have to be very creative if I was going to re-engage nine employees back into the business. While I was excited about my new opportunity, I was also aware that there was a risk attached to the programme – the people on the Ignite team might choose to leave the business at the end of the process. I shared my concern with the management team but the message came back loud and clear that the business was prepared to accept this risk.

I had been through my own journey of re-engagement. Now it was time to take a team of nine disengaged staff through their own process of self-discovery.

Forming the team

When I asked the team managers to nominate one person from their team who they believed was a potential risk to the business and had a perceived reluctance to change, I gave them some criteria so they could select the most appropriate individuals. First, I asked them to observe the behaviour of that person to assess how their performance affected the rest of the team then, to get them thinking, I posed the following questions:

- Who in your team seems to lack motivation and what gives you this impression?
- Who in your team is disengaged and how do you know they are disengaged?
- What negative language do your disengaged team members use?
- Who in your team do you perceive to be arrogant or lazy?
- Who in your team is a disruptive influence and how do you know this is the case?
- Who on your team is behaving in a challenging way and in what ways is their behaviour challenging?
- In what areas of their role are members of your team under-performing and what evidence do you have of their behaviour?

By asking these questions I was able to coach the managers into identifying the right staff for my new team. The questions encouraged them to look for staff who exhibited the kind of behaviour that I knew indicated lack of engagement. Even better, by asking them to look for evidence of that behaviour I was able to ensure that the team members they nominated met my own criteria. Some of the answers they came up with were:

- X has been late on Y occasions with no real explanation.
- X has a high short-term absence record for no apparent reason.
- X has little or no energy when they come into work. It's very rare that I see them smile.
- X is under-performing in Y areas and this has been demonstrated in his/her monthly key performance indicators.
- X never comes prepared to their one-to-ones and shows little or no interest in taking on additional responsibilities or getting involved in personal development.

- X uses language like, "I can't do that", "I won't be doing that" and "I can't be bothered to get involved."

If you ever experience any of these behaviours from your own team, the best advice I can give you is to have an open and honest conversation with them to try to understand what the root cause of the problem is so you can help them identify some possible solutions. Some of the skills that you could use in this situation include:

- Ask open questions starting with who, what, where, when and how.
- Listen and look out for both verbal and non-verbal signs about how they feel when you ask the question.
- Observe their body language: is it open or is it closed? Do they appear to be uncomfortable or too relaxed? What does their body language tell you?
- Build rapport with them and seek to find some common areas of interest. You may need to share some personal information to achieve this, however you will start to earn their trust in the process and this will help you build a relationship with them.
- Never judge your team member or you will lose their trust and respect. What may not seem like be a big issue to you may be significant for them and it is in this situation that they need your support and understanding.

Breaking the news

The next challenge in forming the team was telling the nine who had been selected that they were joining the new Ignite team for the next 12 weeks and that they were going to be working on their self-development. Their managers passed on the news to them and reported to me what response each person gave to it. I was interested to see how each individual felt about the situation. This is a summary of what they said.

- This is just what I need!
- We are the naughty team!
- We are the people that need help.
- Claire's great!
- Claire's harsh, but fair.
- Who is she?
- What can she do that my manager hasn't done already?
- I've never worked with her…
- This is great!

I realised very quickly that each person had a different response to the situation and that each person was already experiencing a range of emotions about being selected. I felt it was important to identify these emotions so I could explore them at a later date. Here is summary of the emotions being expressed at the start of the project.

- I feel anxious.
- I'm frustrated.
- I'm unsure and uncertain.
- I'm confused.
- I'm demotivated.
- I'm disengaged.
- I'm disillusioned.
- I'm ready for a change and a challenge.
- I'm excited.

These thoughts and feelings reaffirmed the behaviour that the managers had experienced with their team members and explained the reason they had been selected for the programme. Crucially, the decision was made from the outset that no one had the right to refuse to join the Ignite team so the challenge for me was to make sure each individual was clear on why they were in the team and what they could hope to gain from it.

Thankfully, the majority of the team saw the benefits of the programme so there were only a couple of people I had to persuade to stay. I promised them that if they remained in the process, the work we were going to do together would benefit them for a long time to come. They could then form their own assessment of the impact that the programme had had on them. I was asking them to trust me and to trust the process that they were going to go through. You can make up your own mind about the success of the programme when you read their success stories in Chapter 6. Do you think they benefitted from the programme and were they right to trust me?

As each person came from a different team and had never worked with the other members as a team before, they were wondering why they were there and what would be different at the end of the 12 weeks. This was a really important stage of the process. If I was going to succeed with them, I knew they were going to have to bond very quickly so they could form into a coherent and close team.

For this reason, it was important that they understood what a good outcome would look, feel and sound like to them at the end of the project. This was likely to be different for each of them and there was a risk that they would not remain within the business once they reached the end of the journey.

Stages of team formation

Forming a team takes time and members often go through recognisable stages of change, moving from being a collection of strangers to becoming a united group with common goals. Bruce Tuckman's model: 'Forming, Storming, Norming and Performing' describes these stages. When you understand it, you can help your team become more effective far more quickly. Let's have a look at this model to see how can you build a highly productive team. You can learn more about the Forming, Storming, Norming and Performing stages from the Mind Tools website at: www.mindtools.com.

Forming

In the Forming stage most team members are positive and polite. Some are anxious because they haven't fully understood what work the team will do, others are simply excited about the task ahead. As a leader you play a dominant role at this point because team members' roles and responsibilities are not clear. This stage can last for as long as it takes for the team to learn to work together.

During this stage you need to get to know your team and encourage them to get to know each other and you, of course. To aid this process, you need to do some team-building exercises. An exercise I use is to hold a team meeting where you ask everybody to bring an item to the meeting that best describes who they are. I then ask them to explain why the object they have brought represents them. When I use this ice-breaker I have seen people bring in every kind of object.

For example, when I did this exercise with the Ignite team, one person brought in an onion. When asked why they thought they were like an onion, they said it was because they had lots of layers and when you strip off one layer you find something new about them underneath. Another person brought in a brick. They said it symbolised the fact that they like to be safe and secure. The brick was their foundation and if you built a relationship with them based on strong foundations then you would build trust at the same time.

The good thing about this particular exercise is that it encourages the team to ask questions and engage with each other on a personal level. It also gets them to develop trust in you, their manager, as well as each other because they have to share something about themselves in order to take part. Any icebreaker is good for a team that is in the

Forming stage because it helps people relax whilst simultaneously pushing them outside their comfort zone.

Other exercises I find useful at this stage of Forming include quizzes and a team night out. One challenge I like to set for the team is called 'getting to know you'. I ask the team who can find out the most interesting fact about the new person. This encourages everyone to get to know their new team member on a deeper level. To make it a bit more fun, I sometimes give a small prize to the person who discovers the most interesting piece of information. All these exercises help the team to feel more comfortable by stripping away layers of their social veneer so they become more responsive to each other.

Whenever you have a new person join the team, you will temporarily go back into the Forming stage as everyone gets to know the new team member. However, you can move through this stage very quickly by using the ice breakers.

Storming

The next stage in the team development process is Storming. This is when individuals start to push the boundaries established in the Forming stage. This is a dangerous time and it is the point at which most teams fail. Storming often begins when there is conflict between team members due to their natural working styles. People work in different ways for all sorts of reasons, but if differing working styles cause issues, the team may become frustrated and angry.

Storming can happen in other situations, too. For example, individuals may challenge the leader's authority or jockey for position amongst themselves as their roles become more defined. If the leader hasn't clearly set out how the team members will work together, individuals can experience a range of emotions, from being overwhelmed by their workload to being uncomfortable with the approach the leader is taking. Some team members may also question the value of the team's goal and so may resist taking on particular tasks. As a result, the team members who stick with the tasks they have been given may experience stress, particularly as they don't have the support of established processes or strong working relationships with their colleagues.

During this stage it is important that you allow the team to express their true thoughts and feelings. The role of the leader is not to judge the individuals in the team, but to seek to understand why they feel the way they do and make them aware of the impact their behaviour is having on the rest of the team.

While to some extent, conflict can be good for progress in knitting the team together, it is important that, as the leader, you notice when team conflict is tipping over into team disintegration.

When conflict arises, you will notice that individuals start to voice their opinions – and they often don't hold back on what they are feeling. This can come across as negative, disruptive and rude. This is probably because the values and beliefs of some members of the team are being brought into question by others. When this happens, it's important that you remember how you feel when someone does not appear to respect your values and beliefs otherwise you may be tempted to gloss over the situation. Take a moment to capture the thoughts that go through your head when this happens to you. How do you behave in these circumstances? How do you feel if someone does not seem to be listening to you? Make a note of what you feel and how you have behaved in similar circumstances. Next, note how your team appears to be feeling and behaving. Highlight the key words you write in your reflective journal because there's a strong chance that your own values and beliefs are also being challenged.

If you notice that your team is in the Storming phase, I strongly recommend you get to the root cause of the disruption and do not ignore the situation and think it will just sort itself out. From my experience, it doesn't just go away, it gets worse. Some leaders avoid any kind of conflict because they struggle to have difficult conversations with team members about their behaviour. But if you want to change the culture and atmosphere of your team, you may need to have some challenging, uncomfortable and difficult conversations.

This is a situation where a coach or mentor can support you. They can discuss what the conversation would look like, feel like and sound like so you are as prepared as possible for it. Your coach will also be there to help you celebrate success when the team comes out the other side of this difficult phase.

Norming

Gradually, conflicts get resolved and the team moves into the Norming stage. This is when people start to resolve their differences, appreciate their colleagues' strengths and respect your authority as a leader. Now that your team members know each other better, they may begin to socialise together, ask one another for help and provide constructive feedback for each other. At this point, individual members begin to develop a stronger commitment to the team goal and the leader starts to see good progress towards achieving it. There is often a prolonged overlap between Storming and Norming because as new tasks come up, the team may lapse back into Storming behaviour again, so there can be a period of overlap between the two stages.

During the Norming stage, observe your team and draw your own conclusions about which stage they are in. Ask yourself who in your team is exhibiting the behavioural indicators of Norming.

1. Who in your team is achieving the majority of their key performance indicators?
2. Who regularly supports others in the team and how do they do this?

3. How do you recognise the achievements and contributions made by your high-performing team members?

It is important at this stage that you recognise all the successes of the team as well as the challenges they face. I normally review this during each individual's monthly one-to-one meeting. I ask them to come prepared with a list of all their successes from the previous month as well as notes about the challenges they face in the month ahead. I then get them to write down all the possible opportunities they have to achieve their goals no matter how weird and wonderful those opportunities may be. I then ask them to pick up to three commitments that we can document as their desired action points for the coming month. I also ask them to think about and consider how these actions will support their development. I then ask where they are in their comfort zone in relation to their actions. It is important that they are stretched, but not stretched so much that they go into panic mode because it all feels too much.

Performing

You will know your team has reached the Performing stage when their hard work leads, without friction, to the achievement of the team's goals. You will also notice that the structures and processes you have set up as the leader support the achievement of goals, too. It will feel easy for individuals to feel part of the team at this stage and people who leave or join won't disrupt performance.

During this stage, the team will be achieving and exceeding the majority of their key performance indicators. As a leader it is important that you delegate as much of your work as possible so you can concentrate on the personal development of your team. Remember, delegation is not an opportunity to dump work on others, it's an opportunity to develop your staff so they grow as individuals as well as part of the team. At this point, the team will have a development plan and each person will be able to articulate how their goals fit with the team's and organisation's goals as a whole.

When you get to this point, your team should be actively seeking promotion and new opportunities to learn. The discussions you have with them should be predominantly about their development and making sure they have the skills, knowledge, attitudes and habits to step into a new role. As a leader you should be encouraging them to keep written notes about where they have made positive contributions to the team's success. There is process for doing this called CAR.

1. **C**ircumstances – What were the circumstances surrounding the achievement?
2. **A**ction – What action did you take to achieve the success?
3. **R**esults – What results did you experience?

If you can get your team into the habit of keeping written notes of how they have made a contribution to the team's successes, it will help them progress in the future. They can use their notes to remind them of what they have achieved and use them as evidence of their ability and skill when applying for promotions and other opportunities for advancement.

Adjourning

Many teams reach this stage eventually. This is especially true for project teams that are only set up for a limited period of time or to achieve a specific goal. Team members who like routine or who have developed close working relationships with particular colleagues may find this stage difficult, especially if their future looks uncertain as a result of the team dissolving. As a leader, it is important that you take time to celebrate the team's achievements as part of the Adjourning process in order to help manage the change. Whenever people leave your team, make them feel special. Organise a night out to celebrate their achievements and thank them for their contribution, and make sure you give them a card to mark the event. It's the simple things that matter in life and a thank you and some appreciation go a long way.

As a leader, think about what you would want others to do to recognise your contribution to the team. How would you feel if your departure went unnoticed? Think, then act accordingly. Keep an eye on team members who go into their shell after the departure of a colleague; they may be struggling to come to terms with losing a close associate or friend. Don't ignore this. Think about what you did during the Storming stage of the team's development. You may need to take similar action at this point and have a difficult conversation with someone about how his or her feelings about the departure of a trusted colleague are affecting both them and the team.

Managing the stages

As a leader, you should be aiming to help your team perform well as a unit as quickly as possible. To achieve this, you will need to change your approach to the team at each stage.

1. Use the descriptions to identify the stage of development your team is in.
2. Consider what you need to do at each point to move the team towards the Performing stage.
3. Schedule regular reviews so you know how your team is progressing and adjust your behaviour and leadership approach accordingly.

Of course, theory is one thing but reality can often be different. Next is a description of how I managed the Ignite team through the stages of team formation.

The Ignite team's journey

When I brought them together, the Ignite team was in the Forming stage, so during our first meeting I made sure that I welcomed each member to the team, acknowledged how they were feeling and told them how excited I was to have the opportunity to work with them and go on a journey of self-discovery with them.

Some of the team had started working for the business at around the same time so, for some, the last time they had been in the same team was during training. It was interesting to see who in the team started to form relationships quickly because they felt comfortable in each other's company, who stayed in the background because they were outside their comfort zone, and who wanted to lead from the front. There were people in the team who knew they shouldn't even be in this situation and they were determined to prove their worth to both themselves and to me.

We were all adults and it was important that I treated them as adults so I allowed them to sit where they wanted in the contact centre. The only caveat I made was that they had to sit together as a team. I told them I was going to sit on the outside of the team so that I could observe what happened on a daily basis. It was important that as a leader I was flying the helicopter so I could see, feel and hear the team moving through the stages of Forming, Storming, Norming and Performing. I also wanted to be in a position where I could step in and move the team quickly through the stages of change, if I needed to. At the end of the meeting I gave them all a red goodie bag containing a journal (so they could capture what they learnt), a notepad and pen, some stress toys and the book, *Who Moved My Cheese?* by Dr Spencer Johnson.

There was just a week between the start of the programme and the formation of the team, which was a lot less time than I would have liked for planning. If I had my time again I would have made sure the programme was in place from the outset so I could move forward quickly with it when the team formed, and I would have made sure that I had had four weeks' notice so I could prepare fully and be ready for all situations rather than flying by the seat of my pants!

Because my senior manager had as clear a vision as I did around the goal of the Ignite team, I felt both inspired and supported throughout the programme so I knew I wasn't on my own with it.

What the programme described in this book does is to give you a structure and a set of tools so you can implement it too. This will give you the confidence to run the programme with different teams in different situations over and over again.

RESOURCES FOR EMPOWERING EMPLOYEE ENGAGEMENT

Go to **www.accendocoaching.co.uk/bonus**

CHAPTER 2
TO CHANGE OR NOT TO CHANGE

I'm starting with the man in the mirror.
I'm asking him to change his ways.
No message could have been any clearer:
If you want to make the world a better place
Take a look at yourself and make that change.
Michael Jackson

Those lyrics have never been more relevant than for this stage in the Ignite Programme because it is at this point that you need to look at yourself and decide whether you are willing to change.

If you are not willing to change, your goal of greater team engagement may not be achievable. However, this is not just about your willingness to change, it's about your team's willingness to change as well. If you are able to accept the discomfort and challenges that accompany change, you will be able to motivate yourself – and lead your team – through the process.

You and your team will experience a range of thoughts and emotions during this transitional period, which is why it is important that you understand the impact of change. This will help you to motivate yourself and support your team through any difficult patches.

Due to the fact that you are likely to get a variety of responses to the work you will be asking your team to do, this chapter is designed to help you deal with each person and situation as it arises.

You first

When any change occurs the first person you need to look at is yourself. Think about a time when you experienced change either at work or in your personal life then write your answers to the following questions in your journal.

- Who instigated the change?
- What thoughts did you have about the change?
- What feelings did you have about the change?
- In your opinion, how did you behave throughout the change process?
- In the opinion of others, how did you behave throughout the change process?
- What were the specific stages you went through? Describe your thoughts, feelings and actions at each point in the process.
- What impact did you have on those around you at the time?
- How did your behaviour affect others?
- If you could have your time again, what would you do differently and why?

As you begin to reflect on your thoughts, feelings and behaviour, seek to understand yourself in more depth. By doing this, you will be able to develop greater self-awareness and this will make you a stronger leader and put you in a better position to understand others.

The mirror exercise

The more you do this exercise the easier it will become, so be patient even if it is difficult at first.

1. Stand in front of a mirror and notice what see, feel and hear (this refers to what you are saying to yourself – in other words what is often referred to as your self-talk).

2. Write down all the good things you see, feel and hear.
3. Next, write down all the negative things you see, feel and hear.
4. Finally, imagine what another person might see, feel and hear then write this down, too.
5. To finish, assess your responses: are you casting a shadow or are you generating sunlight? There is no right or wrong answer to this question – you just need to be open and honest with yourself.

When working with the Ignite team, I asked both myself and the team what the change meant for them. Here is my answer to the question:

> "It's an opportunity for me to demonstrate my leadership and coaching skills. It's an opportunity to prove a concept and gain valuable feedback along the way. I will be totally exposed with nowhere to hide, that excites and scares me all at the same time. I know I am going to go on an emotional roller-coaster and this will be a test of my emotional resilience."

Here are some of the answers given by the Ignite team.

> "I don't like change, but I'll give it a go. What have I got to lose? I might have a lot to gain and it gives me an opportunity to work alongside Claire which I haven't done before."
>
> **Lucy**

> "I'm looking forward to learning something new and hopefully my performance will improve. I am uncomfortable about being with different people, however I do know all of them. I just haven't worked with them before."
>
> **Jack**

> "I really don't know why I am here and what I am going to learn from the experience."
>
> **Andy**

Next, I asked them how they would know whether this was a good change for them or not? Again, I'll start by giving my own answer to this question:

> "I don't know whether it will be a good change or not, however failure is not an option so I am going to give it my best shot and prove how powerful coaching can be when you have the skills and knowledge to deliver."

Here are some of the answers given by my team.

> "Change is as good as a rest. I'm bored at the minute so who knows whether it will be good or not. I've just got to be in the team with an open mind."
>
> **Aaron**

> "I realise I am complacent, comfortable and stale. I come into work, do my job and then go home. What happens if I suddenly lose my freedom and I am constantly analysed? This may be a good thing for me or it could be a disaster waiting to happen."
>
> **Nick**

As the leader of your team, what you have to remember is that change happens all the time. Sometimes it is a big change, like a restructure and other times it is a small change, like someone new joining the team. There will be times when you instigate the change yourself and times when change is passed down from above. Whatever the change, you will need to have the skills and knowledge to lead your team through it effectively. Inevitably, some members of your team will not be engaged in the process so you will need to manage them through it.

As I mentioned in the previous chapter, when you go through change you need to be able to identify where your individual team members are in the four stages of team development: Forming, Storming, Norming and Performing. Those who are not ready for change will very quickly move into the Storming phase and, whether you like it or not, you may need to challenge them about this. That means being prepared to have some potentially difficult conversations with them. As I said before, if feelings are left to fester, disruption will very quickly develop in your team.

Encourage those who are comfortable with the change to bring others along with them by offering support and encouragement, by sharing the positives of the change and helping to reframe any negativity. It is important that, throughout any change process, you effectively communicate what is happening and why. Be open and honest and tell your team what is good about the change and what they will notice as they make progress. For example, your team might notice frowns turning to smiles and energy increasing as more people get onboard with the process. The team will start to have fun so there'll be more laughter and smiles. Everyone will notice that the team is achieving goals and is not afraid to challenge poor performance. The whole team will become encouraging and supportive.

As soon as they start to see the positives of the change, you should hear your team's language change from negative responses to positive. At the same time, you need to be aware that not everyone will see the change as a good thing and you need to respect this, but assure the team that, as the leader, you will support, listen to and encourage them individually. It is at this stage that some people may decide to get off the bus because they don't want to proceed with the journey, and that's fine. However, as the leader you need to help and support them with whatever choice they decide to make.

Remind your team that change creates opportunities as well as challenges, so whether they like change or not, it's an opportunity for them to try something new. All of the Ignite team agreed to go through the change programme and a big part of my role as a coach and leader was to raise their awareness of what they were going to experience along the way. This is something you can do, too.

Mood boards

During the change process, it was important that I was able to make the team aware of the impact that change was having on their feelings. The way I did this was to get them to use a mood board. It was a fun and quirky way to get the team to reflect on how they were feeling and share that with others in the team. The mood board was divided into three zones: green, amber and red. Each day, team members would put their name and an emoticon in one of the zones so the rest of the team could see how they felt. Here is what the three zones and emoticons indicated:

- Bright green with a smiling face ☺ indicated they were happy, motivated, learning new things and feeling positive.
- Amber with a straight face 😐 indicated their mood was changeable. Sometimes they felt happy and engaged but at other times they struggled and felt ready to give up.
- The red zone had a sad face ☹ indicating they were unhappy, demotivated and lacking passion. This was the danger zone.

By making the mood board visible, the whole team could see how each other was feeling and this gave them the opportunity to challenge one another and offer support. As a leader, this was good because I couldn't be with everyone all of the time. It allowed the team to recognise their own and each other's moods so they could work on changing them as a team.

Reflective journal

I use a reflective journal on a daily basis to capture what has gone well throughout the day, and why. It helps me understand what I need to do more of and which skills I need to continue to use and develop. I also use it to capture what has not gone so well (and why) so I can understand what happened and make adjustments the following day. Complete your own reflective journal for a few days before introducing the process to your team. A good way to capture this information in your journal is under the following headings:

- **Successes** – What has gone well and why?
- **Challenges** – What could have gone better and why? I use this as an opportunity to set new goals for the next day.
- **Opportunities** – If you could have your time again, what would you do differently and what outcomes would you expect?
- **Development** – How have you grown as an individual and what have you learnt about yourself? How does this support your career plans?

Self-reflection always needs to start on a positive note so first of all, review your successes. Next, think about the challenges you have faced throughout the day and what it was specifically that posed a challenge for you. Look at the challenge and use it to form a new goal for the next day, making sure it is specific, measureable, achievable, realistic and has a timescale.

Next, brainstorm all the opportunities that have come up during the day, pick two actions you can commit to and use them to help you meet your goal. It is important at this stage for you to capture how this goal fits into your personal development plan and record what can be gained from achieving it. In other words, you need to answer the question: "What's in it for me?" This whole process, if practiced on a daily basis can be finished in around 15 minutes. I complete my own self-reflection journal during my train journey home or before I go to bed at night.

GROW is a goalsetting model that is simple yet effective (for more on this, *see* Chapter 5). Answer the questions associated with each part of the model to help you form and test your goal.

G – What is the **G**oal?
R – Where are you currently (what is your **R**eality) and what is the gap that needs to be filled?
O – What **O**ptions have you got for filling the gap and achieving the goal?
W – What is the **W**ay forward? What actions will you commit to?

It is very beneficial and therapeutic to take time out at the end of a busy day to reflect on what has gone well and why. It slows everything down and will help you clear your mind so when you arrive home you no longer have to think about work. I find this helps me maintain a good work/life balance, which is why I encouraged my team to complete a reflective journal as well. Like a diary, there is no right or wrong way to complete a reflective journal. In mine, I use words as well as pictures because this helps me to use both sides of my brain: the logical and the creative. When completing their own journals, I encouraged my team to capture all of their successes from each day no matter how big or small they seemed. The benefit for the Ignite team was that it:

- Helped them to capture their learnings.
- Slowed down a fast-paced environment and encouraged them to appreciate the moment, in the moment.
- Gave them the opportunity to capture their thoughts and reflect on how their thinking impacted their emotions and, in turn, their behaviour.

- Carved out some time to reflect on their mood and why they might be feeling great – or not – about their achievements.
- Allowed them the opportunity to off-load in a safe environment so they were not carrying any worries around that could affect their performance.

Once you get into the habit of completing a journal it becomes part of the reflection process. What the team discovered was that their moods and behaviour followed patterns and trends. They noted highlights and low moments that they used as evidence for their one-to-one discussions. In short, they gathered proof that the process was having a positive impact on them.

When I introduced reflective journals to the Ignite team, the majority struggled with them at first and I observed a range of responses from "I am comfortable with this and I am just going to get on with it" to "I don't think I'll bother". However, some members of the team found it therapeutic to capture their thoughts and feelings. It helped them see the link between their daily experiences, their goals and their achievements. They later used examples from their reflective journals as evidence of their achievements and results when attending job interviews.

The Personal Transition Curve

The other mood-recognition tool I used with the Ignite team was John M. Fisher's Personal Transition Curve, otherwise known as the change curve. The Personal Transition Curve offers a visual representation of the journey that an individual goes on during any period of change. I used it to show the Ignite team how their emotions and thoughts might alter as they changed their life, their thinking and their behaviour. It helped them to understand the process of change from start to finish and to come to terms with it.

I also used the Personal Transition Curve to help the Ignite team see where they might get to at the end of the 12-week programme if they made the most of the opportunity for personal change and growth. What I love about this tool is that no matter what you are experiencing, you can plot where you are on the diagram and identify how your thoughts, feelings and behaviour relate to where you are in the change process. It allows you to take a look in the mirror and decide whether you are willing to take the next step towards change or not.

Fisher's Personal Transition Curve can be used in understanding both personal and organisational transitions. It is available as a free resource from the website www.businessballs.com where you can also read the theory behind it and explanations about how it works.

Below, I have listed the different stages someone goes through when they progress along the change curve. It gives an indication of what you might encounter from your team as they reach each of the different stages.

- Anxiety – Can I cope?
- Happiness – At last something's going to change!
- Fear – What impact will this have? How will it affect me?
- Threat – This is bigger than I thought...
- Denial – Change? What change?
- Guilt – Did I really do that?
- Depression – Who am I?
- Disillusionment – I'm off! This isn't for me.
- Hostility – I'll make this work if it kills me!
- Gradual acceptance – I can see myself in the future.
- Moving Forward – This can work and be good for me.

The key to using the tool effectively is complete honesty. If your team members are not honest, the only person they will be fooling is themselves. No one wants to be in the depression stage of change, however if that's where you are, that's where you are. You may dislike the fact that this is where you are, but you will have much more respect for yourself if you acknowledge it and use the information to move forward with integrity. By identifying the next step in the change process you might just get the push you need to move to a better place. When working with your team, it's important to remember that we all have a choice about whether to change and we each individually need to decide whether to embrace it or resist it. There is no right or wrong about it, we all have to decide if a change is right for us on a personal level.

Remember, not everyone will want to change. Some people like to play the victim role so choosing to stay where they are serves a purpose. (You can read more about this and the Karpman Drama Triangle in Chapter 3) I had a few victims on the Ignite team. I acknowledged that and I embraced it. I had a choice to make. Am I going to accept this or am I going to seek to change it? What will the team be like if I choose to do nothing? What will it be like if I choose to do something about it? Think about your own team and ask yourself these questions:

- What proportion of my team are mood hoovers? (e.g. they suck all the energy out of me, they're negative Nellies, or they love to be the victim.)
- What proportion of my team are energy givers? (e.g. they are the life and soul of the party with high energy, high enthusiasm and they ooze positivity?)
- What proportion of my team just turn up, do what they need to do and then leave? (e.g. they are reliable, see being 'good' as being 'good enough' and exist in their comfort zones but may be viewed by others as not pulling their weight.)

Take the answers to each of these questions and plot where each individual member of your team is in relation to their comfort zone and the Personal Transition Curve. Next, answer the following questions in relation to your team's level of engagement?

- What might happen if I do nothing?
- What might happen if I make a change?
- What's in it for me?
- What's in it for them?
- What's in it for the business?

I asked the team to plot where they were on the Personal Transition Curve at various points during the Ignite journey. This is where their reflective journals proved useful because what they wrote revealed their thoughts and feelings at particular moments in time. I referred to this information in their one-to-ones so I could continue to help them make progress. Sometimes it was acceptable for them to slip back but what was important for me was that I was able to recognise that this had happened so I could help them refocus and move forward again.

Reading books

If you want to learn more about the change process, it's would be worth reading some of the books listed in the Resources section at the end of this book. Your team might benefit from reading them, too. These books could help you all move through the process of change more easily by explaining the different stages that individuals and teams go through when they are experiencing transitions and challenges. Some of these books are more challenging than others but they all ask you to think about how you personally respond to change and how you can recognise the impact change is having on your team.

The book I find the easiest to read and the one that I find most thought-provoking is *Who Moved My Cheese?* by Dr Spencer Johnson. This book has been used by many corporations who want to get across the message to their staff about change in a more entertaining way. With this in mind, I asked the Ignite team to read the book and then identify which character they identified with most and why. I felt this would give me a good indication of where they were in the change process and what my next step might be.

What I didn't realise at the time was that some of the team would find this task difficult . "Why?" I hear you ask. Very simply, it was because I hadn't established the whole team's preferred learning style. Not all of them had completed the learning preference questionnaire at this point so some of the team struggled to connect with the book. However, this wasn't the only reason. The other problem was that I had asked the team to read the book and connect with themselves. I was asking them to take a hard look at themselves and sometimes they didn't like what was looking back at them. At the point where people are able to accept who they are, they can begin to choose what they like about themselves and therefore identify what they need to do more of. Likewise, they are also in a position to identify what they don't like about themselves and decide whether they want to change. I was starting to push the team outside their comfort zone. Some didn't like this and others loved it.

Working with the comfort, panic and learning zones

There are three emotional zones that we all tend to exist within in relation to change: the learning zone, the panic zone and the comfort zone. Of these, the one we hear about the most is the comfort zone. Your comfort zone expands all the time, this is the place that you feel happiest and least stretched so there is nothing uncomfortable about the comfort zone (normally). When we are growing, we should be in our learning zone as we think about what we are doing and stretch ourselves. I currently spend a lot of time in this zone every day so I know from experience that it can be exhausting and that's why it's important that everyone returns to their comfort zone at times throughout the day.

Understanding the comfort zone

Everyone will have a different experience of being in their comfort zone. However, typically, this is the place in ourselves where we feel safe and secure. It's where we are risk-free and able to relax and experience low-level energy. It is also where we exist through our routines and habits (good or bad) because this means we don't need to think. This could also be a place where we experience boredom. When we are in our comfort zone, we are unconsciously competent or unconsciously incompetent. In other words, we don't know what we don't know. This is a place where we don't think about things.

To understand this better, think about when you're learning to drive: before you even step in the car you are unconsciously incompetent, in other words you don't know what you don't know. When you get in the car you suddenly realise that you don't know how to drive so you become conscious about your driving incompetence. After a few lessons, you know you need to use 'mirror, signal, manoeuvre' before you drive and you consciously think about this as you are driving. Once you have passed your test and have been driving for a while you stop consciously thinking 'mirror, signal, manoeuvre' and just do it so you are unconsciously competent at driving a car.

If you have learnt to drive, you will probably remember the first time you sat in a car and realised you didn't know what to do! In that situation, you were clearly outside your comfort zone. Experienced drivers have the opposite experience: they're so familiar with driving they get in the car and drive. They're so comfortable that they drive without having to think about what they're doing.

Sometimes experienced drivers don't remember the journey home because it is so automatic for them to drive the route.

It's only when we choose to step out of our comfort zone that we need to become conscious and aware again as this is when we need to think. It's important that we take this step because when we do, we step into our learning zone, which is where magical things start to happen. As a leader, it's important for you to recognise when your employees have stepped out of their comfort zone and are unhappy about it as this is a sign that they have stepped into their panic zone.

There was an example of this in the Ignite team with someone I'll call Lisa. When I worked with her, it was quickly clear that Lisa was very unhappy and well outside her comfort zone. Even though she was unhappily outside her comfort zone she was trapped because her comfort zone was so small she had no room for manoeuvre. When we looked at where she was on the change curve she suddenly realised she was in the depression stage of change, and she didn't like it. This was a great opportunity for Lisa to make a choice. She could choose to stay where she was and be unhappy or she could choose to change. You can read her story in Chapter 6, where you'll discover whether she chose to stay stuck in her comfort zone or move into her learning zone where she could change.

Recognising the panic zone

Before we explore the magical learning zone I want to talk about the panic zone. This is the opposite of the comfort zone and the place where we experience discomfort to a level that it causes distress. I have listed what you may find members of your team saying when they are in their panic zone so you are able to recognise it and manage it.

- I can't do this!
- This is horrible / far too uncomfortable!
- I've got butterflies in my stomach.

- My palms are sweating.
- By heart is pounding in my chest.
- I can't think straight!
- My head hurts.
- I feel sick.
- I bet that red rash is moving up my neck...
- I know I'm avoiding eye contact but I just can't help it.

From these descriptions, I'm sure you'll agree that the panic zone is not a nice place to be. Typically, this is where we all have illogical thoughts, display a lot of emotionally-based behaviour and feel; consciously incompetent. In other words, you will know you lack knowledge, skill or ability and this will have a negative impact on your thoughts, feelings and behavior because you are fully aware of your inability to fulfill a task or achieve a goal.

The panic zone presents as many problems for us as our comfort zone, but while we might not notice when we are in our comfort zone, most of us will instantly recognise when we are in our panic zone. The trick for you as a team leader is to recognise both the comfort zone and the panic zone so you can raise your team's awareness of it by sharing what you have observed. Your job is then to move them very smoothly into their learning zone.

Moving into the learning zone

One way to move someone very quickly from their panic zone to their learning zone is to work on their language. Typically, the language of the panic zone is negative. It takes someone into their lesser self, a place where their confidence and self-esteem are low. To get them out of this negative emotional state, I make a note of all their empowered language (in other words their 'can do' language) and compare it to their limiting beliefs (in other words their 'can't do' language). I then ask them to reframe the negative language into positive language. The more limiting beliefs they reframe, the faster they move out of their panic zone and into their learning zone. This is because the negative and emotional language of the panic zone is replaced by the rational thinking of the logical and positive learning zone.

Another method I used to raise my team's awareness of the way they were behaving, feeling and thinking was to get them into the habit of self-reflection. When someone reflects on their thoughts, feelings and actions they move into their learning zone. They become consciously competent., in other words, they become fully aware of the impact of their thoughts and feelings on their behavior and of the positive or negative impact they consequently have on those around them.

Self-reflection offers the chance to gain the awareness of their own behavior they needed in order to be able to change making them constantly aware of the impact they are having on others. To raise your own team to this level of awareness, ask your team if they can recall a time when they felt out of control – explain to them about the example of learning to drive. Find out what was happening for them when they went into panic mode and what they did to calm themselves down. Relate this to the experiences they are having in the team so they can understand how they can use the same calming strategies in relation to their experiences here.

Once someone is in their learning zone they are consciously competent. They know what they are doing, they can articulate it to others and they can express positive thoughts and feelings. This in turn allows them to display positive behaviour and take positive action. So, how do you know if someone is in their learning zone? Here is what you might observe:

- High energy levels.
- High levels of motivation.
- The expression of positive thoughts.
- The expression of empowering ideas.
- The ability to change and explain why.

- Making a positive contribution to the team's performance.
- Showing a high level of skill.
- Demonstrating good levels of self-reflection.

The key to creating engaged teams is to make sure the team are collectively in their learning zone when at work. To achieve this, you need to highlight to your team the importance of taking time out to reflect on their thoughts, feelings and behaviour. The best time for them to do this is when they are in their comfort zone, which is usually at the end of the day when they are relaxing. This was something I encouraged the Ignite team to do and I led by example by maintaining my own self-reflection journal. I still do this today.

When going through any period of change it's important that you focus on keeping your team's energy levels high. When your team's energy levels are high, it indicates that your staff are motivated, engaged and empowered. Similarly, if their energy levels are low, it is probably because your team feels demotivated, disengaged and disempowered. Where would you prefer your team to be on a daily basis? Use these simple tools and you could find that their motivation is higher for more of the time, making them more productive, open to change and development, and willing to take on new challenges and bigger goals. That's a win-win-win, helping you, your team and the business.

The circle of control and influence

We all behave and think as if everything around us is under our control, even though deep down we know it isn't. As a leader, you need to understand what you can control and influence as well as what you can't. That way, you can use your time, energy and resources in areas where you can have an impact, rather than wasting it on lost causes. To help you with this, I'd like to introduce you to another of my favourite tools: the circle of control and influence. It's great because it helps you to quickly identify what is and isn't under your control.

You can introduce the tool to your team as well because it will help them to see what they can control and what is beyond their sphere of influence. This can alleviate a lot of frustration and stop your team wasting time and energy on issues, problems and decisions that are out of their control. By focusing on what they can control, your team's energy will shift so they become more effective and achieve more and better results.

How to create your circle of control

To create your own circle of control and influence, begin by drawing a large circle on a blank piece of paper. Next, draw a smaller circle within the larger circle.

The circle of control

The small circle is your circle of control. Think of yourself within this circle and answer these questions:

- Am I able to change what is happening?
- If I am, do I want to change it?
- When will I make the change?
- How will I make the change?

The circle of influence

The large circle is your circle of influence. Step into this zone and ask yourself the following questions:

- Am I able to influence those who are causing the events I am seeing, feeling and hearing?
- If I am in a position to influence them, who do I need to influence and how will I influence them?
- What do I hope to achieve by influencing them?

When any change happens, whether you are being told to change by the business or you are choosing to change, ask yourself these two simple questions:

- Is this decision within my control?
- Can I influence those making the decisions?

Control is not all about being able to change the source of the change, it's also about whether you are able to control your response to the decision. If you can control your thoughts, feelings and behaviour then you can effectively control and influence the decision-maker. In that case, the world is your oyster.

Once you have identified whether something is within your control or not, you can leave it behind. If something is outside of your control and you won't be able to change it (regardless of what you think, feel and see about it), you will be able to recognise this and move on very quickly. If you don't move on, you could spend far too much time reacting to a decision that is beyond your control. If you think you're getting stuck on something you can't change, you need to ask yourself how much energy you are willing to expend on something you cannot influence or control? What might be the benefits of using this energy on something else? How much better will you feel if you recognise this quickly and shift your thinking? How much time are you going to spend on being angry or upset about something rather than implementing a change or raising concerns about the decision?

When I coach people, I ask them who is in control of their thoughts, feelings and actions. Is it them or someone else? Of course, it is they who are in control. Only they have the power to change what they think, how they feel and what they do – nobody else. It's understandable that we get upset about decisions, changes and events but we need to know how to let go of these emotions so we can perform. Understanding what is in our power to control and influence can help us do that.

The 8 Steps to Success

Before I end this chapter, I want to introduce you to John Kotter's 8 Steps to Success so I can help you take action in relation to your own team, no matter where they are in the process of change. These eight steps show you what steps you need to take to keep moving your team forward towards success.

1. **Create a sense of urgency** – Help others see the need for change and the importance of acting immediately.
2. **Pull together the guiding team** – You need to make sure there is a powerful group guiding change. This group needs to be made up of people with credibility who have leadership skills, communication skills, authority, analytical skills and who are able to convey a sense of urgency.
3. **Create a change vision and strategy** – Clarify how the future will be different from the past and how you can make that future a reality.
4. **Communicate for buy-in** – Make sure as many people as possible understand and accept the vision for change and the strategy for making it happen.
5. **Empower others to realise the change vision** – Remove as many barriers as possible to change so that those who want to make the vision a reality can do so.
6. **Produce short-term wins** – Create some visible, unambiguous successes as soon as possible after implementing change.
7. **Don't let up** – Press harder and faster after the first successes. Be relentless with initiating change after change until the vision becomes a reality.

8. **Anchor change in the culture** – Encourage your team to hold on to the new ways of behaving and make sure they succeed until they become strong enough to replace old traditions.

Below, I explain how I used John Kotter's 8 Steps to Success process in relation to the Ignite team so I could anchor change in the culture of the team and the business as a whole.

Create a sense of urgency

I had the support of the leaders in the business because I had already delivered a presentation on change (based on the 8 Steps to Success). As a result, the team managers knew they quickly needed to nominate someone from their own team to form the Ignite team. My questions helped team managers identify an appropriate candidate, namely someone who was struggling with performance or was displaying negative attitudes and behaviours.

Pull the guiding team together

I was chosen to lead the programme because of my coaching and leadership skills. I had a proven track record of leading a team and addressing underperformance as well as the negative attitudes and behaviours that went with it. I am a good communicator who has authority and I have experience of overseeing the site in the absence of my Senior Operations Manager. I also had the required analytical skills to take the team from good to great and create a sense of urgency about the need for change. I had the advantage of knowing who would be joining me on the programme allowing me to introduce myself and quickly get the consultants together for the team.

Create a change vision and strategy

During the first few days, I communicated the change vision and strategy to the newly formed Ignite team. I told them where they were in terms of performance and described the attitudes and behaviours that had led them to being there. I painted a picture of what the future could look like at the end of the next 12 weeks if they engaged in the process and described the support they would experience on their journey of self-discovery. They knew why they were there and how the end result could look, feel and sound. They also knew they were going on a journey of self-discovery and that this was part of the strategy for success. This was make or break time. They understood they had the power and that it was in their gift to themselves to make that future a reality.

Communicate for buy-in

It was part of my job to communicate the vision and strategy so they understood that they had a choice to stay with me on the Ignite team for 12 weeks or leave the project and carry on as normal, which would result in them not seeing any improvements. Throughout the 12 weeks it was also important for me to communicate to all the key stakeholders (the team managers and Senior Operations Manager) how the team was progressing. I encouraged the team managers to observe coaching sessions so they could improve their skills and increase their knowledge of the programme. Whenever the Senior Operations Manager was on site she would observe what I was doing. This was a great opportunity for me to be coached by her and receive some feedback. It is important to remember that "every coach, needs a coach" and feedback is a gift. During every team managers' meeting I would provide an update on performance and the changes that I was observing. Lack of communication during the change process is a recipe for disaster. This is where most change programmes fail because lack of communications results in a lack of understanding between all the key stakeholders in the venture.

Empower others to realise the change vision

I had been empowered as the coach and leader of the programme. My job was to empower the team and this was achieved through the use of coaching tools and techniques that I introduced to the team on an individual basis. My goal was to make the team feel empowered so they felt enabled to continue to make changes even after the programme had finished.

Produce short-term wins

The Ignite Programme produced a short-term win (12 weeks is short period of time to work within). It was what the team decided to do with their new knowledge that was the true key to success. However from day one, I celebrated successes within the team. I encouraged them to capture their successes, challenges, opportunities and development on a daily basis using their reflective journals. I had praise boards on the wall that I encouraged the team to write on and I delegated responsibility to others within the team so the team as a whole could experience and share success around the team's improving performance.

I provided tips to the team on how they could improve their performance and told the key stakeholders how the consultants associated with the team were having a positive impact on overall business performance and on the attitudes and behavior of the team. The consultants were encouraged to take these short term wins with them when they went back to their teams and share the success with their team managers. This was so the successes of the Ignite team could be shared in the wider arena and in order to encourage the integration of the consultants back into their teams with their managers.

Whenever a member of the team received praise from a customer it was shared within the whole team and across the customer service centre. The sooner you start to celebrate success with your team, the faster others want to be recognised for their achievements, too. Each success is a catalyst for further change and success so that eventually celebrating success and changing the behaviour of those involved with producing it becomes habitual.

Don't let up

No matter how challenging, uncomfortable or risky the 12-week programme felt, I knew I was a woman on a mission – and so were the team. What I learnt about myself was that failure was not an option and I had to face my fear of success. (I was afraid that success would mean I'd no longer need anyone, which would leave me isolated and alone, so I worked on reframing success to represent independence and freedom.) Make sure you don't self-sabotage your success before you reach your final goal.

It was important that the team understood how their individual contribution fitted into the bigger vision on a daily basis so to keep them focused on their progress, I got the team to keep celebrating their successes.

During the goal-setting process I asked them to set goals that stretched and pushed them outside their comfort zone. I explained that a one per cent improvement for each person individually (including me) could add up to a 10 per cent increase in performance across the whole team. That meant if everyone committed to an improvement of just one per cent we would be able to move mountains. If you read the success stories in Chapter 6, you can decide for yourself whether you think the changes implemented during the Ignite Programme were anchored in the culture of the business.

Anchor change in the culture

In this chapter I have introduced you to the tools, techniques, strategies and coping mechanisms you need to encourage and implement change in your team. Change is never straightforward and there will always be challenges along the way. However, you now have the knowledge you need to take on those challenges with confidence and skill.

**RESOURCES FOR
EMPOWERING EMPLOYEE ENGAGEMENT**

Go to **www.accendocoaching.co.uk/bonus**

CHAPTER 3
UNDERSTANDING SELF AND OTHERS

In order to be understood, we must first seek to understand.
Steven Covey

Understanding yourself is really important because if you don't understand yourself, it makes it difficult for you to understand and work harmoniously with others.

This chapter will help you identify those members of your team you are compatible with, and those you are not. Crucially, you will learn that by understanding yourself and others you will be able to manage your whole team and develop productive working relationships with each of them, regardless of whether you naturally get on. This will help you lead and manage everyone to greater levels of productivity and harmony.

There are many different tools you can use as a leader and coach to help you get to know yourself and your team fast. Next, I will show you which tools I used to fully understand my own and my team's communication preferences, needs and learning styles before showing you how I use them as part of the Ignite Programme.

All these tools offer the ability for each of us to gain an insight into ourselves and so they have a huge role to play in the journey of self-discovery that is necessary for change and re-engagement. I recommend that you use these tools within the first four weeks of the programme because the faster you understand your team's preferences the more easily you will be able to adapt your style to meet their needs.

Remember, a good leader always changes their preferences to suit those of the team not the other way around, so learn to speak their language and you will find that they will respond to your initiatives far more quickly.

Once you understand how each of your team communicates, it's a good idea to share this information with the whole team so everyone is aware of the best way to communicate with each other. However, confidentiality is important so make sure everyone is comfortable with having their information shared publically before you go ahead and make it available to everyone. If the team isn't ready to share, create a table so you can capture all the information you need so you can access it quickly and easily for your own personal use when coaching and leading your team. Before introducing the tools to your team, complete each one yourself because you will then have a better understanding of how to interpret your team's results. Understanding yourself is the first step. All of these tools will make getting to know your team faster, making your progress towards engagement faster, too.

Imagine for one moment that you knew how each of your team members prefers to learn and receive information. Imagine that you also knew what motivated each of them and why, how their personalities complement one another and how they could come into conflict with one another. Now imagine how much more effective your conversations with them would be and how much more empowered would you feel by having this knowledge. By using the tools and techniques I describe in this chapter, you will learn how you can access this crucial information so you can use it when working with your team. Let's start by reviewing the first tool, personality profiling.

Personality profiling

Most companies use personality profiling tools to identify whether an individual's skills and abilities match the requirements of a role in the business. However, it is also used to identify whether a particular personality trait is missing from a team. Imagine if all of your team had the same personality traits, the likelihood is you would all go off the cliff together because you would have no one to bring you back. It's important to remember that you need a mix of people in every team so you have access to a range of different strengths when taking on challenges and tasks. As your team will be a mix of different personalities, skills and abilities, it means you can all learn from each other as you grow and develop as a unit.

There is a wide variety of personality profiling tools available, including Myers Briggs, Belbin, Insights, and Tetra Map to name but a few. Personally, I use DISC, which combines the key aspects of most of the profiling tools. However, each categorises people into one of a range of profile outlines using a symbol such as a colour (Insights), an element (Tetra Map), an object (Belbin) or letters (Myers Briggs and DISC) to indicate which profile someone fits into.

Personality profiling tools are used to identify a range of personality types. The tests categorise different traits which are each identified by a letter, colour, object or element. It's important to remember that these categories are generalisations so the description used to describe a personality type may or may not fit someone perfectly.

The main benefit of a personality profiling tool is that it gives you an insight into someone's key personality characteristics and preferences. This allows you to understand them quickly rather than having to spend months getting to know them. It's especially useful if you are working with people for a short period of time, as I was with the Ignite team.

Personality profiling can also help you and your team members identify each other's key strengths as well as where each other might need additional help or support. I will share my own personality profile from DISC so you get a sense of the kind of information you can glean from using such a tool.

My profile description and category

My profile category combines I and D on the DISC tool, showing I am outgoing and people-orientated rather than reserved and task focused. My personality profile description reveals that I predominantly use an influencing style and approach when managing and working with others. I am not afraid to share my opinion but I am able to back it up with a story or evidence.

However, in a stressful situation I can be impatient as this is when my 'hurry up' gene comes out to play. This moves me away from the people-focused attitude that is my natural and preferred approach to working with others. My tendency towards impatience needs to be taken into consideration when I work with others on stressful projects as I can become dominant and demanding. Others need to be aware that this is how I respond to pressure and that it's not necessarily a criticism of their work. While 'dominant and demanding' are not the way I want to be, I recognise that these traits play a vital role in business and in my own coaching practice because they can get me through difficult situations and help me to see a task through.

As you can see from this, DISC gives you information about yourself and offers you an opportunity to use this to your advantage so you can choose to change as and when you feel it is appropriate.

DISC – Personality Profiling

DISC is a psychometric test that is affected by ENVIRONMENT and measures the needs-driven portion of our personality. It is a profiling system that opens the door to communication and that can be highly effective in helping to build better relationships through effective communication. The questionnaire takes around 15 minutes to complete and from this a report is generated that summarises someone's personality. This can then be used to form the basis of an individual development plan.

DISC can identify:

- Motivational drivers.
- Preferred environments.
- Goal-setting preferences.
- How an individual may set out to achieve goals.
- Decision-making strategies.
- How an individual likes others to communicate with them.
- How an individual prefers to communicate with others.
- An individual's greatest fears.
- Areas where an individual may feel challenged.

As well as all this, DISC also identifies whether an individual is outgoing or reserved and task or people focused. Once you know this, you can adapt your style to suit them and so have more productive conversations and more harmonious working relationships with them. How many times have you heard the saying 'opposites attract' or 'we get on so well because we are like two peas in a pod'? If you sat down and identified the differing personalities in your team, you would be able to work out why you get on well with some of your team and not so well with others. It is probably because of your different personalities.

If you use a personality profiling tool, you will soon be able to identify who in your team prefers detail and why they like it. You will quickly be able to see what the implications and impact would be if you didn't give a detail-orientated person a lot of nitty-gritty information. You will also be able to identify who in your team would be happy to get started on a task with minimal information. Imagine if you asked a detail-orientated person to work with someone who prefers less detail. Do you think they would work well together or do you think there would be conflict?

The report that is generated for each team member by the profiling tool would explain exactly how different personalities work together and why, as well as highlighting the potential problems and challenges you might face if you paired some different personality types together. As I have previously mentioned, you need a mix of all the personalities in your team so that you can use their strengths to get different types of tasks done.

Imagine if you had a group of people who needed everything to be perfect before the task was complete. If they were working on a project together it would probably never get finished. Likewise, if you had a team of creative, imaginative people who were great at generating ideas, there would be nobody to make any decisions so the project would lack direction. From these examples, you can probably see how a profiling tool could be very effective in helping you to manage your team. It will allow you to play to your team's strengths, help you identify their individual needs and allow you to communicate more effectively with them on a one-to-one basis.

It is equally important that when you have a mix of personalities in your team you all understand each other's personality type so you can all learn from each other and grow as a team. Where one person needs to learn and develop another could help them because they have the necessary skills. When the two individuals work together this could be a very powerful and effective combination as their skills and personalities complement each other. It would be very empowering to have one person's need for development recognised as an opportunity for growth when the right people work together in the right environment.

For example, you may have someone in your team who is creative but lacks organisation (making their work quite stressful for both themselves and others). If they were asked to work with another member of the team who was well-organised they could learn new ways to manage their workload and get more done. Equally, the organised team member may have the opportunity to learn how to be more creative and follow through with their ideas. Each person could learn from the other, which means they would both be able to develop.

I don't want to give too much away about the personality types in case you decide to try it for yourself, but to give you a flavour of how different personalities are identified, here is a little taste of the kinds of personality traits that are identified by DISC.

- **D** – Dominant, Demanding, Decisive, Delegates – Do it kind of person – Outgoing and Task-focused.
  For example: Simon Cowell.
- **I** – Influential, Inspiring, Positive, Energetic, Charming – Outgoing and People-focused.
  For example: Sir Richard Branson.
- **S** – Sympathetic, Steady, Seeks Harmony, Organised, Kind – Reserved and People-focused. For example: Mother Theresa.
- **C** – Conscientious, Critical, Creative, Analytical, Perfectionist – Reserved and Task-focused.
  For example: Michael Jackson.

Can you see how certain people with different traits could clash while other types might get on extremely well? Can you also see why you need at least one of each of the character types on a team in order to make it a success? Remember, if you have a team where everyone has the same personality-type – or is dominated by one type – the whole team could go off the side of a cliff together.

Learning styles

It is important to understand the different learning styles of those in your team because this allows you to deliver training solutions in a way that suits each of them best.

This means they will respond to the training better and learn faster. By understanding the individual learning styles of your team, you will be able to manage each of them more effectively.

Personally, I like to learn by being told what I need to know so I have the chance to ask questions before trying and testing a method myself. When this happens, I am more engaged in the training and I'm firmly in my learning zone. I feel empowered because it feels as if someone knows me and is respecting my learning preferences.

Today, businesses are using e-learning more and more as their main method of delivering training. This is great if your employees prefer to learn by reading and interacting with technology but it's not so great if they don't. While I understand that e-learning is cost-effective and convenient, it's important to recognise that it won't work for everyone. If you have someone on your team who struggles to learn by reading, test them about what they have learnt as soon as possible after the training otherwise the key messages may be lost. This is especially relevant if the training has pushed someone into their panic zone (where their thoughts and feelings will be illogical and irrational) or if the training has pushed them into their comfort zone (when they will become bored with the whole learning environment and won't engage with it at all).

Honey and Mumford's Learning Styles

As you have just seen from DISC, everyone has a different personality profile and the same is true for our learning profile. This is why I used Honey and Mumford's Learning Styles tool with the Ignite team. The questionnaire is designed to discover someone's preferred learning style and it helped both me and the team understand their learning preferences. To take the test, each team member had to quickly answer a questionnaire made up of 80 statements. Speed was critical as it was important that they answered with their gut rather than their intellect to prevent them from over-analysing their responses. The questionnaire is available online if you want to use it with your team.

Over the years, you have probably developed learning habits. These habits lead you to benefit more from some learning experiences than others. Since you are probably unaware of your habits, the questionnaire will help you pinpoint your learning preferences so that you are in a better position to select learning experiences that suit your natural style. Next, let's explore the four different learning styles identified by Honey and Mumford in more detail.

Activists

Activists involve themselves fully and without bias in new experiences. They enjoy the here and now and are happy to be dominated by immediate experiences. They are open-minded and unlikely to be skeptical so this means they are often enthusiastic about anything new. Their philosophy is, "I'll try anything once." They dash in where others tend to hold back and in the process of doing that they throw caution to the wind. Their days are filled with activity. They revel in short-term crises and fire-fighting, and they tackle problems by brainstorming so as soon as the excitement they get from one activity has died down they are busy looking for the next. They tend to thrive on the excitement of new experiences and get bored when it comes to implementation and longer term consolidation. They are gregarious and enjoy it when they are constantly interacting with others. This means they tend to hog the limelight. They are the life and soul of the party and seek to focus all activities around themselves.

How to communicate with an Activist

When communicating with an Activist, keep things brief. So be bright and be gone. Make sure you don't give them a lot of detail and allow them to learn from their mistakes and experiences. They need to learn by trying something for themselves and coming to their own conclusions. After they have had a chance to try something out, have a quick chat with them about what went well and what didn't go so well, and then let them try again. You will know if you have an Activist in your team because they are like whirlwinds in the office, constantly moving from one thing to another. They frequently multitask and often have numerous applications open on their computer.

Reflectors

Reflectors like to stand back and think about experiences. They prefer to look at situations from many different perspectives, collect data (both from firsthand experience and elsewhere) and chew over what they learn thoroughly before coming to any conclusions. They like to ensure they have a complete collection of data before beginning their analysis so they tend to postpone reaching conclusions for as long as possible. Their philosophy is to be cautious, to leave no stone unturned and to 'look before you leap'. They like to 'sleep on it' rather than taking immediate action. They are thoughtful people who like to consider all possible angles and implications before making a move. They prefer to take a back seat in meetings and discussions because they enjoy observing others in action. They listen deeply and like to understand a discussion before pitching in with their own opinions. They tend to adopt a low profile and have a slightly distant, tolerant, unruffled air about them. When they act it is as part of a wider picture that takes account of the past as well as the present, and their own observations.

How to communicate with a Reflector

When communicating with a Reflector, allow them time to think. Silence is powerful and it will be both comforting and empowering for a reflector. They will feel that you are allowing them the time they need to consider their thoughts and responses, which feels very respectful for a reflective learner. If you ask to see their reflective journal you will find that it is full of insights into their thoughts, feelings and actions. By reading it, they will feel good that you have taken time out to share their experiences. Don't get frustrated that they take a back seat, instead ask for their opinion 24 hours after an event. This is when they will be able to share their true thoughts because they will have had time to 'sleep on it'. Remember this phrase as it's a good one to use with a reflective learner.

Theorists

Theorists adapt and integrate their observations into complex but logically-sound theories. They think problems through in a vertical step-by-step and rational way. They assimilate disparate facts into coherent theories. They tend to be perfectionists who won't rest until things are tidy and subsumed into their ordered scheme. They like to analyse and synthesise data. They are keen on basic assumptions, principles, theoretical models and enjoy system-based thinking. Their philosophy prizes rationality and logic and their theory is, "If it's logical it's good". Questions they frequently ask are, "Does it make sense?", "How does that fit with that?", "What are the basic assumptions here?"

Theorists tend to be detached, analytical and dedicated to rational objectivity rather than anything subjective or ambiguous. Their approach to problems is consistently logical. This is their 'mental set' and they rigidly reject anything that doesn't fit with it. They prefer to maximise certainty and often feel uncomfortable with subjective judgements, lateral thinking and anything flippant.

How to communicate with a Theorist

The most effective way to communicate with a Theorist is to ask lots of questions so they can explain the theory about something and how it works in practice. You have to be prepared to go into detail with these types of learners. You will also need to clarify and summarise key points so you are both on the same page. Don't be surprised if you have a detailed and fully-formed action plan after speaking with a Theorist. Imagine if you were an Activist in a team of Theorists. You might want someone giving you information to be brief, be bright and be gone but the Theorists could be there checking the facts for hours! How frustrating would that be? If it happened to you, how would you manage your state? Alternatively, you might like to think about how useful a Theorist could be in your team, especially if you were naturally an Activist.

Pragmatists

Pragmatists are keen on trying out new ideas, theories and techniques to see if they work in practice. Pragmatists positively seek out innovative ideas and revel in taking the first opportunity to experiment with new applications. They are the sort of people who return from management courses brimming with ideas that they can't wait to put into practice. They like to get on with things so they tend to act quickly and confidently on ideas that attract them.

Pragmatists don't like 'beating around the bush' and tend to be impatient with ruminating and open-ended discussions. They are essentially practical, down to earth people who like making decisions and solving problems. Typically, they respond to problems and opportunities as if they are a challenge. Their philosophy is, "there is always a better way" and, "if it works, it's good".

How to communicate with a Pragmatist

When communicating with a Pragmatist, focus on the experience. Ask questions like, "What have you learnt?", "How will you implement this learning?" and "When will you implement the learning?" When they return from a learning experience such as an event or training, they will just want to get on with the job, which means you will see action as well as reflection. As long as a Pragmatist thinks the way they want to do something will have a positive impact they will implement what they know. If they are in any doubt, they will look for another way to achieve and deliver a result.

Learning from the learning styles

Which of the learning style profiles resonate most with you? What have you learnt about yourself and your team just from this brief introduction to the learning styles outlined here? Would it surprise you if I told you I was predominantly a Pragmatist/Activist according to the Honey and Mumford Learning Styles test? You can probably see now how this influenced me in deciding to take on the challenge of the Ignite team. For me, taking on the team was exciting. It was new, it had never been done before, and failure wasn't an option so it was right up my street! What opportunities have you accepted that fit with your own learning profile and how has your own learning preference influenced the way you approached the task?

Do you remember how in the very early stages of the programme I asked everyone in the Ignite team to read *Who Moved My Cheese?* I already knew how some of the team was going to respond to the activity – who would love it and who would struggle with it – because of the answers they had given on their learning styles profile questionnaires. This is what I observed from studying their behavior at the time.

- One third of the team was fairly comfortable and got on with reading the book. They finished it in 30 minutes and enjoyed it. They understood its relevance and why I'd asked them to read it. They were quite happy to discuss their observations with me in the team environment. They even laughed and shared examples of why they connected with a particular character. This enabled me to quickly identify some of their personal goals so they could start to change.

- One third of the team reluctantly read the book but it took almost the entire day for them to do it. They felt stretched and challenged by the task but they knew the challenge wouldn't go away so they decided it was best just to get on and do it.
- The remaining third went into their panic zone when I asked them to read the book and as a result decided not to read it at all – it was just too much of a challenge for them. They didn't see the benefit of reading the book so they procrastinated.

It was clear from this that the Activists were keen to find out what was in the book rather than reading about it. However, I knew the Theorists would love reading the book but would struggle to put it into practice. Being a Pragmatist myself, I knew I would prefer it if someone else did the reading and told me what I needed to know so I could implement the ideas because even though I can still read and implement, it's a slower process for me. The Reflectors would have liked to read the book, process the information, sleep on what they had learnt and discuss it 24 hours later.

Now, I could have simply chosen to ignore the fact that one third of my team didn't read the book, but what message would it send to everyone else if I did that? I decided to speak to each of the people who didn't read the book so I could understand why they found it such a big challenge. I also wanted to know what they were experiencing when they went into their panic zone.

What I discovered was that one of the employees suffered with dyslexia so asking that person to read a book stirred up a lot of emotion from school and memories about how he struggled to read. His past experiences made him feel demotivated when it came to reading the book. He knew he was being disruptive but the pain he was experiencing was too great to allow him to modify his behaviour. Because part of his role involved him reading scripts to customers, this issue with reading was a very real problem for him. However, fortunately I discovered this problem early on in the Ignite programme so I was able to make sure he had what he needed to perform in his role. This goes to show how important it is to understand your team, their learning styles and their issues, otherwise they will never be fully engaged and they will never perform in the business.

Once you have understood your team's learning preferences, you need to start doing some work to find out what their communication preference is too. This is important as it will have a big impact on how you deliver information to them. The easiest way to identify your team's communication preferences is to understand VAK.

VAK preferences

VAK profiles (Visual, Auditory or Kinaesthetic), indicate which senses individuals like to use when learning i.e. do they like to be talked to, do they like to see images or do they like to learn by doing? While it is important to understand someone's learning preferences, I believe it is also important to understand how they prefer to receive information or how they prefer someone to communicate information to them. Once you know if someone prefers material to be delivered using visual, audio or kinaesthetic methods, it will allow you to adapt your training, language and presentation style to match their requirements.

This is really useful when building rapport. There is nothing worse than asking a visual person a hearing question, you instantly lose rapport. For example, for a visually-led person, rather than asking, "How does that *sound* to you?", ask "How does that *look* to you?" I have a natural preference for both visual and kinaesthetic learning, but I've developed the habit of asking, "So, what will you see? What will you hear? What will you feel?" so that all the key sensory preferences are included.

So, how do you know whether you – or your team – have a preference for visual, audio or kinaesthetic learning? Surprise, surprise! There is a questionnaire you can fill in to help you find out. It is made up of 30 statements each with multiple choice answers. Depending on whether you choose mostly A, B or C shows whether you prefer to use your visual, audio or kinaesthetic senses most.

To complete this questionnaire, you need to go to www.businessballs.com where you can download it for free. Below is a detailed description of what each learning style involves and how you can allow for it when you pass on training, information and project details to your team.

Visual

Someone with a visual learning preference likes to see or observe things such as pictures, diagrams, practical demonstrations, displays, handouts, films, flipcharts etc. These people will use phrases such as "show me", "let's have a look at that" and will be best able to perform a new task after reading the instructions or watching someone else do it first. These are the people who will work from lists, written direction and instructions. Within a team environment, you are likely to have a lot of visual displays highlighting successes, challenges and opportunities. Providing a vision board to someone who is visual is a great way to encourage them to capture their goals using both words and images. When working with a visually-led member of staff, you should use questions like, "What does success look like to you?", "Describe what you will see when your goal is achieved" and "Show me your vision board". In a meeting you may find that they draw diagrams or doodles representing their ideas or have lists of actions they will be working on when they get back to their desk.

Auditory

Someone with a preference for learning by listening is auditory. They have a preference to get information by listening to others speak, hearing themselves speak or listening to other sounds and noises. These people will use phrases such as "tell me", "let's talk it over" and will be best able to perform a new task after listening to instructions from an expert. These are the people who are happy being given spoken instructions over the telephone and can remember all the words to songs they hear. Within a team environment, they might have music on in the background or they may have headphones on as they listen while they work. They would prefer to talk things over and speak their thoughts out loud. Giving them technology so they can record themselves or others speaking would be great for them. They could then listen to their own voice recordings or recordings of what others have said while travelling into work, for example. When coaching someone with an auditory preference, you need to use questions like, "What does that sound like?", "What will you be hearing people say when you have achieved your goal?", "What does success sound like?" In a meeting they would be equally happy talking to the audience or listening to a presentation.

Kinaesthetic

Someone with a kinaesthetic learning style has a preference for learning through physical experience such as touching, feeling, holding and doing; in other words, practical hands-on experiences. These people will use phrases such as "let me try", "how do you feel?" and will be best able to perform a new task by going ahead, trying it out and learning as they go. These are the people who like to experiment and take a hands-on approach. They will probably not want to look at written instructions first. It's important when coaching a kinaesthetic learner that you ask them questions like, "What does success feel like?", "How does that make you feel?" and "What will it feel like when you have achieved your goal?" In a meeting, make sure they have something that they can play with that won't distract others. Stress balls are a great tool for a kinaesthetic learner because they can play with it while listening and talking.

VAK and the Ignite team

When the team came together on the first day of the programme, everyone was given a goody bag containing a mix of tools to assist any learning style. The bag consisted of the following:

- Note pad and pen.
- Reflective journal.
- Stress toys.
- The book, *Who Moved My Cheese*.
- A ring binder in which they could keep their tools and performance results.
- Balloons.

Although most of us commonly have one main preferred learning style, we usually use all three learning styles. Some people have a stronger preference for one style than another whereas other people have a more even mixture of two or (less commonly) all three styles.

Having implemented the Ignite Programme in a call centre environment, I expected the majority of the people on the team to have preference for auditory learning but I was wrong, which just shows how dangerous assumptions can be in business.

Eighty per cent of the team had a preference for visual learning, which meant it was vitally important that they had visual displays to highlight key messages, performance results and successes. I was now beginning to understand why active listening was so weak in the team and the impact this was having on many of the team's personal performance. Because active listening was such a vital skill in their telephone-based role, I was starting to understand where and why they were under-performing and how they had ended up in the Ignite team.

It was important that as the leader and coach of the team that I listened out for key phrases the team used and adapted my language to suit their preferences. I also highlighted to them when they had actively listened to their customer and what impact that had had on the customer's experience of speaking to them. By adapting my language to match each team member's preference, we had much more effective one-to-one meetings and team discussions.

All this new knowledge I gained from the completion of DISC and the learning style questionnaires was having a positive impact on the relationships I was building with the team because we were communicating far more effectively with each other. This resulted in trust and respect being developed quickly between us, all of which helped with the re-engagement of the team back into the business. All this happened because they finally felt they were understood.

The zones and motivation

Motivation occurs when you step outside of your comfort zone. When you are in your comfort zone you experience comfort, security and boredom so it is unlikely that you will feel motivated. You are more likely to do nothing and just relax. When you are in your panic zone you experience discomfort, stress, anxiety and irrational thoughts so the likelihood of being motivated here is also slim.

When you are in your comfort zone, you are more likely to procrastinate because you cannot control your thoughts and because you like the sense of comfort. That means you are more likely to do nothing. It is your responsibility as an individual to move out of your comfort or panic zone and into the learning zone, which is where you grow. When you are in this area, you will feel motivated to achieve your goals.

As a leader, you have a responsibility to motivate your team. You are responsible for recognising where your team is currently residing in relation to their comfort zone and make them aware of it. When your team is in the learning zone and displaying signs of motivation, it is your responsibility to understand their motivators and play to them. By doing so, you can support, encourage and inspire your team to achieve both their own and the team's goals.

Once you are aware of how you can influence, inspire and engage your team, more of your business goals will be achieved. Someone only becomes motivated when they choose to step out of their comfort zone and stretch themselves. This is why you need to understand what motivates your team so you can help them take that step. When I shared this information with the Ignite team they were surprised (to say the least). I asked the whole team to complete a motivation questionnaire to help me understand what motivated them. Key motivators are normally captured in one word such as money, security, recognition and achievement. Usually, these words are connected to core values. You can use both motivators and values to understand how to encourage your team to step out of their comfort zone and become motivated.

It is important that you understand the meaning of the words your team uses to describe what motivates them because it could mean one thing to you and something completely different to them. It is important that you question your employee so you understand what they mean by the word 'motivation'. This will allow you to make sure that you're both on the same page and speaking the same language. There is a questionnaire to help you do this and you can get it online as a free download from my website at www.accendocoaching.co.uk. There are other motivation-defining questionnaires available online too and I have also used the Motivation Pillar tool (available from www.motivationalmaps.com).

This is how I used the motivation questionnaire with the team. I asked the Ignite team to rank the following 12 motivators in order of importance with 1 being the highest motivator and 12 being the lowest.

1. Independence
2. Recognition
3. Achievement
4. Leisure Time
5. Power
6. Prestige
7. Money
8. Pressure
9. Self-Esteem
10. Family/Social Life
11. Security
12. Personal Growth

Of course, motivation is critical to success, but it is just as important to understand what demotivates someone as it is to understand what motivates them. For example, a member of your team might be motivated by recognition but demotivated by prestige. So if they are recognised in a public arena, it could demotivate them rather than motivate them. If recognition is someone's highest motivator but prestige is their lowest, avoid recognising their achievements in public.

When setting goals with an employee it's also useful to check whether and in what ways the goal is congruent with their personal values and motivators. If the goal isn't linked to a key personal motivator the employee is likely to remain in their comfort zone because the goal will not stretch them enough. It's vitally important that you know this because it could be the difference between having a team that is engaged and having a team that is disengaged.

By understanding an individual's needs, you will be able to manage them individually as well as part of the team. The more you know about someone, the more effective you will be as a leader and this knowledge will enable you to ignite your team for peak performance.

Maslow's Hierarchy of Needs

Maslow's Hierarchy of Needs is often used to determine an employee's level of satisfaction with their role. It's a great visual tool, too and it can be used to establish where people are in relation to their current mood.

For any team to work, the foundations have to be in place before it can become highly engaged. I used Maslow's tool with the Ignite team as a way of gauging where people were on a daily basis so I had an idea of what they were thinking and feeling as well as how they were behaving. Maslow's Hierarchy of Needs is available as a free download.

As you can see from the diagram below, the base of the triangle is SURVIVAL. It is followed by SECURITY then BELONGING, IMPORTANCE and finally at the top of the triangle is SELF-ACTUALISATION. Below is a description of what each step signifies and the impact it has on individuals, organisations and even whole countries. Look at the triangle and imagine what you would be seeing, hearing and feeling at each step on it.

Survival

- I'm only here for the money.
- I'm leaving as soon as I can.
- I'm not satisfied with the job I do.
- My work doesn't excite me.
- I'm a clock-watcher.
- I'm a jobs worth.

It's fair to say that in this part of the triangle, employees would be disengaged, look unhappy and have little energy. In other words, they would just be plodding through the day. Guess what? I had some of those in the Ignite team. I identified them easily by just looking at their faces and listening to what they said. I drew their attention to what I saw and talked to them about the impact this was having on the team as a whole.

Within the first four weeks of bringing the team together, I started to talk to some of them about how unhappy they looked. Having people in your team who are just there for the money and intend on leaving the business as soon as possible can be soul-destroying for others. This is because the behaviour of unhappy people can be destructive. That's why it's important that you don't ignore it simply because you're afraid that a conversation might lead you to saying, "I'll help you find a role in another company that excites you." Sometimes the right thing for all concerned is to have that conversation and help those team members move on, even if it means they leave the business or company entirely.

Security

- I'm interested in overtime.
- I have more sick days than I should.
- I have poor working conditions.
- I don't like my manager or working in my team.
- I don't like my job much, but I get on with it.
- I read job ads.

It's fair to say that employees in this section of the triangle are not engaged and they still have sad faces because they are demotivated. Guess what? I had some of these in the Ignite team too! Once again it is important to identify these people. You need to tell them what you see in order to raise their awareness that their behaviour is obvious and is having an impact on those around them. This is like giving them a mirror and saying, "Have a look yourself, what do you see looking back at you?" You could get their absence records and show them what it looks like on paper, especially if you have identified any patterns, like the fact that they frequently take Mondays and Fridays off sick. Here, you would question the employee to seek to understand what is going on in their lives that is affecting their behaviour.

Doing this will undoubtedly be challenging but if this was your business would you want to continue paying a salary to someone who was off work a lot or who didn't seem to want to be there? The likelihood is they are motivated by security so they stay in their job even though they don't like it. They are too comfortable and they need moving out of their comfort zone and into their learning zone where they will grow.

Belonging

- I know I'm part of something bigger.
- I like it here some days, other days I don't. Some days it's fun, other days it's boring.
- I'm proud to work here but I wouldn't necessarily shout it from the roof tops.
- I might leave if I'm tempted.
- There are no career development programmes here.

At this point, you will be starting to see, sense and hear evidence of engagement. When people get to the middle of the triangle, they are almost engaged. At the start of the 12-week Ignite Programme I had at least two people who were already engaged. Within four weeks, I had moved the majority of the team to the Belonging section of the triangle. I did this by talking to them on a daily basis and using all my coaching skills to question them, listen to them, build rapport with them and set goals with them that would move them forwards. This is a really important stage and if they are not supported at this point, they can quickly move backwards again. As the team leader, it is part of your role to keep your team moving forward. Apart from anything else, when you do this it will increase engagement because your team will know you are truly interested in them and that you want them as part of your team. In other words they'll feel they belong and that they are important, which is the next level on the hierarchy.

Importance

- I'm a vital part of the business.
- I feel important at work.
- I'm really busy but I also feel I'm stretched and able to grow.
- I'm an achiever.
- I'll only leave if something much better comes along.

It's fair to say that when your team is here you will see smiles on their faces, and sense a high level of energy, enthusiasm and motivation. Personally, I was at this stage when I took on the Ignite team and the challenges they represented. I was aiming to get myself to the top of the triangle while bringing the rest of the team with me, too. Here, employees are engaged in the business and would score positively on employee engagement tests.

Remember that employees can move up and down the levels of the triangle quickly so throughout the whole process you need to work with your team to ensure they stay engaged. It's easy to forget people when they reach the level where they feel important because you know that they are performing. As a leader, the majority of your time is probably going to be spent with the under-performers because they are the ones that cause you a problem. However, by spending time with those on your team who feel important means you will be delivering results across all key performance indicators. As a leader, this will give you a lot of positive energy and motivation while also helping you develop skills that support your own growth.

Self-actualisation

- What can I do for others?
- I inspire others to do their best.
- I love working here!
- I'm a high flyer!

Only a small minority of any team – on average less than 15 per cent – will reach this level of engagement. These employees are recognised as the high flyers in a business. How many do you know in your organisation? What is it that they do on a daily basis that allows them to be the best? As a direct result of the Ignite Programme, I am now perceived throughout the business as one of those 15 per cent. I am delighted by this, however it hasn't happened by chance; it is the result of sheer hard work, determination and my decision to be my brilliant best every day.

Once the team has reached the Belonging and Importance level they are either almost engaged or actually engaged in the business. If you have good employee engagement results, it means that the majority of your team is in the top three sections of the hierarchy.

Understanding relationships with PAC

We all have relationship habits or stances that we use when we interact with each other. As you grow as a leader, you will need to become aware of your own stances and those of your team if you are going to challenge, change and develop them. The PAC model, developed by Thomas A Harris in his book, *I'm OK, You're OK* reveals how we have a tendency to fall into the roles of Parent, Child and Adult when we relate to specific people in our lives. For example, a member of your team may take on Child behaviour in relation to you, but Parent behaviour in relation to a colleague and Adult behaviour in relation to his or her own children.

You need to understand the relationship paradigms so you can work on altering them. Below is a description of each of the behavioural patterns so you can identify the behaviour pattern before seeking to change it. The ultimate goal is for your whole team to have adult to adult conversations so that everyone is empowered and engaged and therefore able to work together in harmony.

Parent

The parent predominantly ***tells*** someone what to do, but they can also be the ***rescuer*** in a situation. The problem with this is that it stops the person being rescued from learning and doing something different next time. Thomas Harris describes the mental state defined as "Parent" as a collection of "tape recordings" that are stored then replayed in response to external influences. These recordings are based on what a child has observed adults around them doing and saying. The recording is a long list of rules and admonitions about the way the world is and how the child is expected to behave. Many of the rules are useful and valid throughout life, others are simply opinions that may be less helpful.

Parent is a state in which people unconsciously think, feel and behave in a way that mimics the way their parents or other parental figures acted or the way they interpreted their parent's actions. For example, a person may shout at someone else out of frustration because they learned this behaviour from an influential figure in their childhood.

Child

The Child state is one in which people behave, feel and think in a way that is similar to when they were children. The Child predominantly behaves like the ***victim*** and will live in a ***blame*** culture. They are likely to say, "It always happens to me", "It's not fair" and will sometimes cry as a form of release. Just as the parent's voice is a collection of recordings, so is child's. It retells the internal events of how life felt when the person was a child. Harris suggests that when, as adults, we feel discouraged, it is as if we are reliving our Child experiences even though the stimulus of the parent may no longer be relevant or helpful for us.

For example, a person who receives a poor evaluation at work may respond by looking at the floor, crying or pouting as if they are being scolded like a child. Conversely, a person who receives a good evaluation may respond with a broad smile and a joyful gesture of thanks. The "Child" is the source of emotions, creativity, recreation, spontaneity and intimacy.

Adult

The ***Adult*** has those difficult, challenging, open and honest conversations which can at times mean they are the ***persecutor*** whereby the person on the receiving end doesn't like what they hear and has to make a choice about how to respond to the information being conveyed. An Adult's intention will always be good and as a result it can have a positive impact. However, it can also have a negative impact if it is not well-received. This happens when the receiver is in Victim or Child mode, in which instance the Adult will be perceived as a persecutor.

According to Harris, children start to develop the third mental state of Adult, at about the same time as they learn to walk and begin to achieve some measure of control over their environment. Instead of learning ideas directly from parents or experiencing simple emotions as the Child, children begin to explore the world and form their own opinions. They test the assertions of the Parent and Child and either update them or learn to suppress them, thus the Adult inside of us all develops over time, but is very fragile and can be readily overwhelmed by stressful situations.

Adult is a state of the ego which is most like an artificially intelligent system that processes information and makes predictions about major emotions that could affect its operation. Learning to strengthen the Adult is a goal. While a person is in the Adult ego state, he or she is directed towards an objective appraisal of reality.

Along with the Karpman Drama Triangle, the PAC Model allows me to make a member of staff aware of their behaviour. The Triangle is useful because it is a visual tool that can be understood quickly and easily.

The Karpman Drama Triangle

The drama triangle is a psychological and social model of human interaction developed by Stephen Karpman in 1968. It models the connection between personal responsibility and power in conflicts, and the destructive and shifting roles people play. As a tool, it is frequently used in psychotherapy, especially in transactional analysis. Karpman used the triangles to model conflict or drama in intense relationship transactions.

He defined three roles in the relationship: Persecutor, Rescuer (the one up positions) and Victim (one down position). Karpman placed these three roles on an inverted triangle and referred to them as being the three aspects, or faces of drama. Karpman chose the term 'drama triangle' rather than 'conflict triangle' as the Victim in his model is not intended to represent a victim of violence, but someone experiencing the victim state.

- **The Persecutor** insists "It's all your fault". They are controlling, blaming, critical, oppressive, angry, authoritative, rigid and superior.
- **The Victim** is of course persecuted. The Victims stance is "Poor Me!" They feel victimised, oppressed, helpless, hopeless, powerless, ashamed and seem unable to make decisions, solve problems, take pleasure in their life or achieve insight. The Victim if not being persecuted will seek out a Persecutor and also a Rescuer who will 'save' the day but also perpetuate the Victim's negative feelings.
- **The Rescuer** has the line: "Let me help you". A classic enabler, they feel guilty if they don't go to the rescue. His or her rescuing has negative effects though as it keeps the Victim dependent and gives the Victim permission to fail. The rewards derived from the Rescuer role are that the focus is taken

off the Rescuer. When he or she focuses their energy on someone else it enables them to ignore their own anxiety and issues. This Rescuer role is also very pivotal because their actual primary interest is really an avoidance of their own problems disguised as concern for the Victim's needs.

Can you think of a time where you have played one of these roles? What was the impact on you and others? Spend some time now reflecting on your behaviour.

- Can you think of a time when you have seen these traits in your team?
- What did you do?
- Knowing what you now know, what would you do differently?

My role as the leader of the Ignite team was to identify throughout the 12 weeks when and if they played any of these roles and then use my observations to have open and honest conversations about them. If I was going to move them forward and continue to build their trust I had to be confident in my findings, knowledge and ability and I had to demonstrate that I knew what I was talking about.

You now have a variety of tools you can use daily to begin advancing your team towards greater levels of engagement and performance. The next step is to align this with your team's individual values and beliefs so they can raise the level of their performance within the business.

RESOURCES FOR EMPOWERING EMPLOYEE ENGAGEMENT

Go to **www.accendocoaching.co.uk/bonus**

CHAPTER 4
VALUES AND BELIEFS

Change your thinking, change your behaviour.
Claire Cahill

Your team member's values and beliefs have a huge impact on the way they think, feel and behave. And it is those values and beliefs that influence the way they perform. If they have positive beliefs about themselves and what they can achieve, their performance is likely to improve. But if they hold negative beliefs about themselves, they will be limited and this will have a negative impact on their performance. In this chapter, we will discover what beliefs and values are and how they are formed. You will also learn how to elicit your team's values and beliefs, and once you have done that, learn how you can use this information to positively influence performance on an individual and team level.

If you want to understand your team's values and beliefs you need to build good rapport with them. That way, they are more likely to trust you and share their view of things. It is important that they feel safe enough to be open and honest with you. Due to the fact that your team members are sharing their deepest thoughts and feelings, you need to reassure them that anything they share is in the strictest confidence. If there is anything you want to share for the benefit of the rest of the team, make sure you agree it with them beforehand. Trust is critical when working with your team on their values and beliefs because in order to change their idea of what they can achieve and how they can change, you will have to challenge them, and you cannot challenge them if they don't trust you.

Understanding beliefs

We all have positive and negative thoughts. Negative thoughts are often referred to as limiting beliefs and positive thoughts as empowering beliefs. By helping your team change their limiting beliefs into empowering ones you will be supporting their personal growth. What you will usually find is that once they experience this change in their beliefs, they will be more willing to share their thoughts and feelings with you. This means you can build an even greater level of trust with them and help them grow even faster. First, let's explore what beliefs are and how they are formed.

1: When do you develop your beliefs?

Many of our beliefs are instilled in us by the time we are seven years old. They include beliefs about our worth as individuals and what we can achieve. These beliefs often stay with us throughout life. However, there are some other beliefs that we discard. Let me give you some examples.

- Did you believe in the tooth fairy?
- Did you believe in Father Christmas?

How old were you before you started to question whether these beliefs were true or not? I was probably about 10 years old when I started to question the existence of Santa and the tooth fairy. Now, of course, I know they don't exist, but I still ask my own children to believe in them because they are magical and enthralling.

But why do we abandon beliefs in fantasy characters but not negative beliefs about our worth or ability? The simple answer is that our beliefs in Father Christmas and the tooth fairy are challenged (otherwise we'd be a laughing stock) while deeper beliefs about our self-worth have never been questioned. So it is possible for us to change our beliefs when they become unhelpful, inappropriate and when they are challenged by ourselves and others, but often that simply doesn't happen.

Values and beliefs are typically handed down to us by our parents, siblings, teachers and through our faith, culture and social organisation. They are what we believe to be true because others have told us so or because we have had them instilled in us from an early age. However, we all interpret what we have learnt differently, so although we use the same word for a value e.g. respect, it could mean something different to each of us depending upon what we have been taught about it. It is important when challenging the values and beliefs of your team that you do not judge someone based on their interpretation of a word (value). Seek to clarify what it means to them even though it may mean something different to you.

2: How do you identify a belief?

A belief is an idea you hold as true. You form your belief based on what others tell you and what you experience for yourself. Once you start to think something is true, you go about looking for evidence to support your belief because for you, it is true. There may be no evidence for it whatsoever but once you develop a belief, you will imagine or make up evidence for it because it serves your purposes. After all, your whole view of the world is based on what you believe to be true.

3: How do you elicit beliefs?

Whereas values are encapsulated in one word, beliefs are usually expressed as statements and are often formed into a short phrase or sentence. As an example, here are some beliefs I have held myself or heard others expressing.

- I'm no good at sales.
- I will never be as good as X.
- I don't have the confidence to do X.
- I've always been rubbish at X.

- I've always been bottom.
- I'll never earn a bonus.
- I'll never get a promotion.

These are all negative beliefs that limit thinking and negatively impact performance because they prevent someone from even making the effort to challenge the status quo. Your task as the team leader is to help your staff change their negative beliefs into more empowering ones that will help them achieve their goals.

It's worth carrying a notebook or blank piece of paper when you're around your team so you can make a note of any limiting beliefs you hear them express. Look out for what they say and who they say it to. What is the impact of that phrase on the person saying it? What is the impact on other members of the team, on the customers and on the business as a whole? When challenging the person who expressed the belief, ask them the following questions:

- Do these beliefs help or hinder you in achieving your goal?
- Do these beliefs empower or limit you?
- Where do these beliefs come from?
- What evidence do you have that this belief is true?

I got into the habit of noting down my own beliefs and asking myself these questions on a daily basis when I was with the Ignite team. I then made a record of what I found in my reflective journal.

4: How do you interpret and use the information?

Imagine if you had the skills and the confidence to help change your employees' belief systems? What impact would that have on your team's performance? How much more successful would you be as a leader? Imagine what it would feel like to hear your team say:

- I believe 110 per cent that I can achieve it.
- I know I can finish in the top three and be on the podium celebrating success.
- Nothing is going to stop me now!
- I have the confidence to deliver X.
- I will secure X sales by month end.
- I have the confidence to have difficult conversations with X.
- I am good, and good is good enough.

These beliefs are empowering and even more importantly, they support the achievement of goals. It's important when creating goals that you have a record of the empowering beliefs each member of your team has expressed. You can then draw their attention to the times when they have expressed those beliefs so they can see the positive impact it had on their performance and feel the magic in them. When you notice your team expressing their beliefs, let them know what you are seeing, feeling and hearing in the moment because this adds further credibility to the empowerment process. I did this with all of the Ignite members and the results were amazing.

Understanding values

Just as you learnt to understand your team's beliefs, it is important that you get to know their values as well. If you do this, you will understand what motivates them and this will make it easier for you to engage and inspire them both as individuals and as part of the team. As you start to delve a little deeper into your team's values, you will discover that each of them uses a number of words to describe what they value. This is important, because once you know what words they use, you can begin to find out what those words mean to them. It is important that you excavate that meaning so you get a more detailed and accurate picture of what is at the true heart of their values. Remember, good communication with your team will lead to greater rapport and trust.

1: Where do your values come from?

Whereas beliefs are formed as the result of experiences and what we are told by others, values are exclusively passed on by others such as parents, siblings, friends, colleagues and organisations. Our values are what drive us to do what we do. They also have a direct impact on our motivation and this in turn impacts our performance. The more deeply you understand your own or someone else's core values the more you will be able to help them raise their performance and improve their results. In a work environment, when personal and company values are compatible or mutually supportive, the individual and the business will achieve the best possible outcomes.

2: How do you identify a value?

A value is typically expressed as a single word such as honesty, family, security, growth, respect. In the same way, the word we use to describe what motivates us is also usually encapsulated in a single word. Often, the word we use to describe our values and the word we use to describe our motivation are one and the same.

3: How do you elicit a value?

I use a values elicitation tool called "Ultimate Beliefs" that has been developed by Pam Lidford from The Coaching Academy. This helps me get to the root of what a value means to a member of my team. In summary, you ask your employee to write down their core values.

You then take each separate value and ask what it means to them specifically and whether it is a positive or negative value (in other words, does it help them achieve their goals or does it stop them from achieving their goals). You need to continue the questioning until your employee has identified their top three values. These are otherwise known as their core values.

To give you an example of how a value can be negative or positive, I'll share my value of 'security'. When doing a values elicitation, I identified that I had a desire for security. On the negative side, security can keep me rooted to the spot and prevent me from moving forward. But on the positive side, when I feel secure, I am able to launch myself forward from a firm platform. As I need to feel secure before I can take a risk, security is a value that works in my favour. It allows me to take calculated risks because when I believe I'm secure, I'm able to take action.

To be honest, I never wanted security to be one of my core values, but when Pam Lidford elicited them in front of a crowd of 100 aspiring coaches, I had to accept it. Even though I am aware that it can both help and hinder me, I sometimes experience internal conflict and discomfort as my need for security both holds me back and helps to drive me forward. That said, knowing I have this value has helped me to make decisions much faster because I understand how it plays out for me both positively and negatively.

4: How do you interpret and use the information?

The only way you can interpret your team's values is by listening to them carefully (*see* 'Building trust through active listening' later in this chapter). When eliciting someone's values, you need to begin by writing down the values they express and what those values mean. You can keep a record of these meanings and their top three values in their one-to-one document or in your personal learning journal. They can then make a note of what they have learnt in their own personal learning journal, too. Using this information, you can make sure you talk their language when you communicate with them because this will show that you truly understand what their value means to them.

Once you are aware of your own values you can begin to understand how they can help or hinder your performance as a leader (through goal-setting and developing leadership qualities) as well as that of your team. You will also be able to understand how your own values align with those of the company you work for. Conflict arises when your personal values and those of your company don't match. This lack of congruency between personal and corporate values is one of the main reasons why employees leave a business. The pressure exerted by a mismatch of values creates overwhelming conflict that is too much to handle because they relay the message that, "I am unable to remain true to my authentic self". It is your role as a leader to talk to your staff if their values are not aligned with those of the business, otherwise you will never understand the issue or be able to help. Ultimately, if an employee's values cannot be aligned with that of the business, it may suit both parties if the employee leaves.

Why do values and beliefs matter?

Values and beliefs are significant because they play a big part in making you who you are as an individual. They drive you to exhibit certain behaviours and perform particular tasks, whether those actions are helpful or not. Sometimes your team will have no idea why they do what they do. That's why so it's important that you have the knowledge and skills to be able to raise their awareness of their positive or negative values so they have a better understanding of their own internal motivation.

It is also important that you take time out to reflect on your own personal values and beliefs and how they may differ from those of your team. This is because your awareness of your own values and beliefs will have an impact on your relationships and your ability to inspire, motivate and encourage your team to achieve peak performance. I used my journal on a daily basis so I could capture my own personal values and beliefs and discover how they helped or hindered the performance of the team. Doing this gave me the opportunity to change my approach to situations quickly and challenge my own values and beliefs.

Active listening

One of the skills a leader has to develop is active listening. How many times have you heard yourself saying "Yes" and "No" in all the right places without properly taking in what is being said to you? Is this really listening or have you just heard what someone has said? Listening is one of the most important skills you can develop because it has a major impact on your effectiveness and on the quality of your relationships with others.

- We listen to obtain information.
- We listen to understand.
- We listen for enjoyment.
- We listen to learn.

Given all the listening we do, you'd think we'd all be good at it! In fact, most of us are not and research suggests that we remember between 25 per cent and 50 per cent of what we hear. That means when you talk to your boss, colleagues, customers or spouse for 10 minutes, they pay attention to less than half of what you say. How does that make you feel? Turn it around and it reveals that when you are receiving directions or are being presented with information, you aren't hearing the whole message either. You hope the important parts are captured in your 25-50 per cent, but what if they are not?

The way to improve your listening skills is to practice active listening. This is where you make a conscious effort to not only hear the words that another person is saying to you, but to understand the deeper message being conveyed. In order to do this, you must pay attention to the other person very carefully. You cannot allow yourself to become distracted by whatever else may be going on around you, and you cannot get immersed in forming counter arguments you want to make when the other person stops speaking. You also cannot allow yourself to get bored and lose focus on what the other person is saying. All of these contribute to a lack of understanding.

Building trust through active listening

I have previously mentioned that listening is a skill that needs to be learnt and developed, and the only way you can do this is with daily practice. When coaching my team, I have to make sure that I am actively listening to everything they say and don't say. During our one-on-one sessions, I make copious notes so I can refer back to details in our conversation and remind them of what they said to me. This allows me to explore their thoughts and feelings through further questioning so I understand what specific words and statements mean to them. Some of the questions I ask are:

- Tell me what you mean by X.
- Give me an example of what X looks, feels and sounds like.
- How will you know when you have X?

Listening is a vital skill in facilitating this process. By listening carefully, you demonstrate that you are genuinely interested in what the other person has to say and that you can hear the deeper message they are sending you. When it comes to talking about values, you can share with your team member when their interpretation of a value matches yours, however it is important that you do not try to push your interpretation of a value onto them. Instead, thank them for sharing their views and make sure you remember their interpretation for future conversations.

During a one-to-one session, it is important that your team member feels able to express or vent their emotions to you in order to process their negative feelings and get to a place where they are ready to be positive again. Holding on to negative emotions can be destructive for individuals as well as those around them, which is why it's good to build a strong open, honest and trusting relationship with your team through active listening. Remember that as the leader of your team, you need to be completely non-judgemental and impartial otherwise your team will not feel able to talk to you.

How to engage in active listening

There are five key active listening techniques, all of which help you to make sure you are hearing what the other person is saying to you, and that reassures the other person that you are hearing what they are saying.

1: Pay Attention

Give the speaker your undivided attention and acknowledge what they say. Recognise their verbal and nonverbal communication. Look at them when they are speaking to you, set aside any distracting thoughts you have, don't mentally prepare a response and avoid being distracted by environmental factors such as conversations that are going on around you.

2: Show you are listening

Use your own body language and gestures to convey that you are listening by nodding occasionally, smiling and using other facial expressions. Make a note of your posture and make sure it is open and inviting. Encourage the speaker to keep talking by using small verbal comments like "yes", "okay" and "uh huh".

3: Provide feedback

Our personal filters, assumptions, judgments and beliefs can distort what we hear. As a listener, your role is to understand what is being said. This may require you to ask questions. Reflect what is being said by paraphrasing, e.g.

"what I'm hearing is" and "it sounds as if you are saying". Ask questions to clarify certain points e.g. "What do you mean when you say…?" and summarise the speaker's comments periodically to check you have understood their meaning correctly.

4: Defer judgment

Interrupting is a waste of time. It frustrates the speaker and limits your full understanding of the message. Allow the speaker to finish each point before asking questions and don't interrupt with counter arguments.

5: Respond appropriately

Active listening is a model for respect and understanding. You are gaining information and perspective. You add nothing by attacking the speaker or otherwise putting him or her down. Be open and honest in your response, assert your opinions respectfully and treat the other person in a way that you think he or she would want to be treated.

It takes a lot of concentration and determination to be an active listener. Old habits are hard to break and if your listening skills are, like many people's, not well-developed you will need to work hard to develop the necessary skills. If you find yourself responding emotionally to what someone says to you, say so and ask for more information e.g. "Maybe I'm not understanding you correctly but I find myself taking what you said personally. What I thought you said is xxxx; is that what you meant?"

Be deliberate with your listening and remind yourself that your goal is to truly hear what the other person is saying. Set aside all other thoughts and concentrate on the message. Ask questions, reflect and paraphrase to ensure you understand what is being said. If you don't, you'll find there is a big difference between what someone says to you and what you hear.

Listening is a skill that we can all benefit from improving. By becoming a better listener, you will improve your productivity as well as your ability to influence, persuade and negotiate. What's more, you will avoid conflict and misunderstanding. All of these are necessary for building trust and workplace success.

Top tips for effective active listening

- If you're finding it difficult to concentrate on what someone is saying, try repeating their words mentally to yourself or writing them down. This will reinforce the message and help you stay focused.
- Use body language and other signs to show you are listening. A simple nod of the head will remind you to pay attention and not let your mind wander.
- Try to respond to the speaker in a way that will encourage him or her to continue speaking so that you can get the information you need. Questioning and recapping what has been said also communicates that you understand what you are being told.

Of course, when messages are communicated to us verbally, if we listen we will know what is being said to us. However, a great deal of information is non-verbal, conveyed through tone of voice, body language or is contained in what is *not* said. By understanding the Iceberg Model, you will be able to discern some of the less obvious messages that are being conveyed.

The Iceberg Model

Our messages are like icebergs: a very small amount of what we think and feel shows up as language. What you see above the surface doesn't always reflect what is happening or has happened below the surface. Like the ice below the surface of an iceberg, the beliefs and values that we hold – and which have such a big impact on what we think, feel and do – are often invisible. Once our personal values and beliefs have been triggered, we have thoughts and these, in turn, stir emotions. When this happens, it's as if the iceberg that is usually below the surface begins to emerge above the surface and become visible. When your team member's values and beliefs rise to the surface, you will be able to see them through their behaviour.

If their beliefs are empowering and their values are congruent with the company's values, your staff will probably have had positive thoughts resulting in positive emotions. If this is the case, you should witness positive behaviours and results.

On the flip side, if any members of your team have limiting beliefs or their values are in conflict with the company's values then they will probably have negative thoughts, which in turn will stir negative emotions. The consequence will probably be negative behaviour, which can be extremely disruptive and have a negative impact on the business.

As a leader, you will need to challenge your employee's values, beliefs, thoughts and feelings if they are having a negative impact on the team and the business. You have to be the catalyst for change, even though this may feel alien or uncomfortable to you. Here are some of the consequences that may be experienced by you, the team and the business if you fail to challenge negative thoughts and behaviour.

- As a leader: there are many potential consequences of ignoring what goes on beneath the surface of your team members' mind. First of all, if you don't understand what is going on in someone's head you will ultimately end up ignoring what they are feeling. As a result, they will probably exhibit negative behaviour and their performance will be negatively affected, too.

- For an employee: there are going to be consequences if their poor performance is not addressed. The employee will think that their contribution is acceptable and this could lead them to become more challenging to you as the leader, especially when you come to review their performance at annual appraisals and discuss potential pay increases. This could cause conflict that might have been avoided with earlier intervention.
- For customers: the consequence of allowing negative thoughts, feelings and behaviours to continue in your team is poor service. This means there are likely to be complaints made against the business. This in turn will impact you as a leader because it will be your responsibility to deal with the lack of customer satisfaction. This conflict could easily have been avoided if you had tried to understand what was going on in your team member's mind.

By now you can see that managing poor behaviour is challenging but rewarding as it helps your employees grow and develop as individuals.

What you have to remember is that your team will have beliefs that have been instilled in them since the age of seven. Although every individual has a choice about whether they change those beliefs, as a leader you have a responsibility to shine a light on them so you can challenge those beliefs and help your staff member discover whether they are empowering or limiting. By doing this, you can raise your staff's awareness of their values and beliefs and the impact that these have on both themselves and the team. Beliefs can be changed and, when used to their full advantage, they can be extremely empowering. Once a leader and employee are empowered, the iceberg will soar into the sky. Who knows how successful the team could be when that happens!

How to raise awareness of beliefs and values daily

Here is quick summary of what you need to do on a daily basis in order to raise awareness of your team's values and beliefs so you can facilitate greater motivation, improved performance and better results.

1. Always carry a notebook and pen with you so you can capture the values and beliefs you hear, see and feel being expressed by your team.
2. When talking to your team, actively listen to what they are saying, observe their body language and also notice what they are not saying.
3. Question your team to get a better understanding of what their values mean to them. Use this information to raise your team's awareness of their values and whether those values help or hinder them in achieving their goals.
4. Support your team in changing their limiting beliefs into empowering beliefs and capture these on a visual display so the whole team knows what you are trying to achieve.
5. Agree what the core values of the team are with everyone in it and capture those values on a visual display so the whole team is reminded of them.
6. Encourage the team to be open and honest with each other so you create a safe environment for sharing. This will build their confidence that they will not be judged for their thoughts and feelings even if they are then challenged in a positive way.
7. Highlight how values, beliefs, thoughts and feelings in the team impact behaviour and how behaviour affects the team's results and the customer experience.

The iceberg model in action

Thinking back to my team member who had dyslexia and the reading challenge I set with the book *Who Moved My Cheese*, it became clear that he did not intend to be disruptive and cause a scene by saying, “No, I’m not doing this”. The impact of that task caused him discomfort and pain, but I had no way of knowing this because it was all going on beneath the surface in his thoughts and feelings. What I did experience though, as did others in the team, was his negative statement that “I can’t do this and I am not doing this”. In other words, this was the only expression of his reluctance to complete the task. Others in the team then said, “This isn’t fair, we felt uncomfortable but we still did it. I thought we were all here to learn.”

Suddenly conflict was being created within the team as the thoughts, feelings and emotions of other members of the team started to come to the surface. Once I had spoken to the dyslexic team member about his behaviour and gained his permission to share his situation with the team, the storm calmed down. As a result of this, the whole team understood his behaviour and they quickly became supportive rather than resentful. This also helped to build trust within the team because everyone was allowed to share their issues. In effect, I was giving them all permission to be vulnerable.

This shows how important it is that employees and managers recognise and understand their own and others’ behaviour. It’s easy to understand that if one member of the team leaves their negative thoughts and feelings inside, this negativity can have a detrimental effect on everyone else in the team. Likewise, if your team expresses positive thoughts and feelings then as the team leader, you need to ensure they are radiated throughout the whole team so everyone can share them. Positive thoughts and feelings create positive behaviour, which is powerful.

Challenging conversations

The desire for change cannot come only from you, it must come from your team as well or there won't be any progress. Enabling someone else to change their behaviour means you will need to challenge them, and that means having open and honest conversations that both you and your staff member may find difficult. However, it is only by having these conversations that you start to discover what is going on for someone on the inside. Just for a minute, imagine you are a fly on the wall observing your team then answer the following questions:

- What behaviour are you seeing?
- Would you say your team is exhibiting a high, low or medium level of energy?
- What conversations are you hearing?
- Is your team making positive or negative statements?
- What banter do you notice between your team members?
- Would you describe it as healthy or stale?

It's important that you take time out throughout the day to complete this exercise. If things are going well, celebrate this and be part of it, after all as the leader you have made this happen. If you decide there are issues or negative behaviour you need to address, take it up with the member of staff in question by having a challenging conversation.

- How confident do you feel on a scale of 1-10 in having a challenging conversation with an employee who is disengaged in the business?
- What are you going to do to raise their awareness of the impact their behaviour is having on the team?

Preparing for challenging conversations

Before going ahead with challenging conversations with your team, you need to prepare. Remember the 5Ps: Proper Preparation Prevents Poor Performance (Charlie Batch). Think through your answers to the following questions so you are fully prepared:

Where are you going to have this discussion?

The environment you choose to have any conversation will have an impact on it. At this point you probably have no idea how your team member is going to react to the conversation that is going to take place. You are likely to be discussing an emotive subject so make sure you have tissues available in case they get upset. They may also get angry, so talk in private as you don't want to cause a scene in front of the rest of your team. They already have you as an audience so make sure there is nobody else as a witness to their feelings. What they have to share may be extremely sensitive or confidential and they may be embarrassed so give them time to process their thoughts and respond to your questions.

What do you want to say?

Work this out carefully so you feel confident and in control before you begin the conversation.

What are the key points you want to get across?

Again, get clear on what these are before your meeting and decide how you are going to present them.

What evidence do you need to gather before the conversation takes place?

Keep some written notes so you can be specific and accurate when addressing particular incidents. There is nothing worse than not having all the facts to hand during a discussion. As the leader you are a credible force so this is key to your success.

If possible, keep things brief. These discussions can take a matter of minutes when you are clear on what you want to discuss and the message you want to get across. A lot of time can be wasted if you skirt around the issue.

When raising someone else's awareness of their behaviour, you want the employee to be focused on solutions not problems. If the solutions come from them, they are more likely to implement those ideas because they own them. They will be empowered by this and feel encouraged because they will be thinking for themselves. What powerful questions could you ask? Remember, you want them to do the thinking but you need to be able to provide relevant information and prompts in case they get stuck. Make sure you are fully prepared with some killer questions as these can get to the bottom of issues quickly. Here are a few powerful questions to get you started.

- What could be affecting your performance?
- How do you know this is the case?
- What do you think about your current business performance?
- What's your view of your current business performance? (Good if they are visually led.)
- How do you feel about your current business performance? (Good if they are kinaesthetically led.)
- How does that make you feel?
- What needs to change for you to be able to improve your performance?
- What help and support do you need in order to make it happen?

Sometimes, just having a few questions prepared, listening closely and knowing what you want to talk about will enable you to come up with the most relevant questions. Some of the best questions I have asked have come in the moment when I have truly understood the person in front of me and I am genuinely interested in them.

By now you should have done sufficient observations and reflections to understand the correlation between the intent and impact of your employee's thoughts and feelings on their behaviour. You should have some questions to get you started when having challenging conversations. By being a role model, being prepared to change your own behaviour and by addressing the behaviour of your team, you will demonstrate that you are prepared for a challenge and that you are not afraid to do yourself what you ask of others.

If you come up against a problem with recognising and understanding behaviour, don't be afraid to be vulnerable and ask for help. There are coaches, mentors, peers and consultants who would be more than happy to help and support you. Remember a day without learning is a day wasted. This is a great opportunity to grow and shine so seize the moment to unlock your own potential as well as that of your team.

RESOURCES FOR EMPOWERING EMPLOYEE ENGAGEMENT

Go to **www.accendocoaching.co.uk/bonus**

CHAPTER 5
GOALS AND VISION

Set a goal that is so BIG, so exhilarating that it EXCITES you and SCARES you at the same time.
Bob Proctor

I love this quote from Bob Proctor because it is so simple and so effective. When you set yourself a goal it has to be so big it takes you far enough outside your comfort zone for your motivation to kick in. However, to avoid internal turmoil and fear getting in the way, your goals need to be congruent with your values. Before helping the Ignite team to set their goals, I knew it was important that both I and they had done the work to understand what motivated each one of us and that we all knew what our values were. Having explored my team's motivators and values I was able to assist them in setting goals so I could help them understand their "WHY" – the reason for setting those goals in the first place.

"The real value of setting goals is not the recognition or reward, it's the PERSON WE BECOME by finding the discipline, courage and commitment to achieve them."

(Anon)

As well as clear, congruent goals, all teams and groups need a vision of where they want to get to, otherwise they will have no idea where they are going, what needs to be done or how and when to celebrate their successes. That's why, in this chapter, you will learn how to create a vision so you can a create goals that drive both you and your team forward.

"If you don't know exactly where you're going, how will you know when you get there?"

Steve Maraboli

Team and company vision

All organisations have a corporate vision, an aspirational description of what the organisation wants to achieve or accomplish in the short, medium and long terms. This vision provides the company's employees with a clear direction and gives them missions to complete within a set time period. When I formed it, my intention for the Ignite team met the company's vision of 'increasing employee engagement and enablement'.

What is a vision?

All good leaders have a vision and when I began working with the Ignite team, I did too. In his famous book, *The 7 Habits of Highly Effective People*, Stephen Covey wrote that one of the founding 'habits' is "to start with the end in mind".

As a coach and team leader, this is what I encourage too, so it was only right for me to begin here when working with the Ignite team so I could create a clear vision of what 'the end' looked like. My vision statement for the Ignite Programme was:

> "To take a team of people and improve their performance from good to great over a 12 week period. To empower a group of people who are currently disengaged, demotivated and disinterested by addressing under-performance, attitudes and behaviours and motivation levels by taking them on a journey of self-discovery using coaching tools and techniques."

My plan

A vision can't work unless there is a well-formed plan supporting it to become a reality. My vision for the Ignite Programme helped me decide which tools, techniques and approaches I wanted to use in order to make it a reality. Here is a summary of the tools I decided to use and the approaches I wanted to take.

- Use Bruce Tuckman's stages of team development theory (Forming, Storming, Norming and Performing) to guide and manage my team.
- Get the team's buy-in to the project by sharing ideas.
- Believe that my vision can be achieved and convey this to the team through the message: "Let's prove we can do it together" that was born of my natural influencing style ('I' on DISC).
- Demonstrate honesty and courage, which are two of my leadership traits.
- Create a visual display with lots of positive quotes to inspire and encourage the team on their journey.
- Continuously question myself as the leader of the team on how I could get the best out of each individual.

My next task was to work out how I was going to bring the vision to life. My solution: through building trust. There are a variety of skills, tools and techniques that can be used to do this but here is a summary of the tools I decided to use to build trust with the Ignite team.

DISC

By using a personality profiling system, I could get to know people in minutes rather than months. By doing this I was able to adapt my communication style to suit the needs of each individual on my team. This increased rapport and helped me to develop a trust-based relationship with each person on the team.

Communication Cycle

Listen to what someone is saying then seek to check your understanding by asking questions, clarifying what you have heard and repeating back what you have heard. Finally, agree a way forward and offer support and encouragement.

'Connect then lead' flowchart

There are two ways we assess others as trustworthy, first we ask: "Can I trust this person?" (A test of warmth). Secondly we ask: "Can I respect this person?" (A test of competence or strength). Leaders need to demonstrate both warmth and strength to succeed. However, leaders who project strength before warmth risk eliciting fear in their team rather than trust. The best way to build trust in a team is to begin with warmth because this facilitates good communication and makes the team more willing to take on new, different or challenging ideas. As a leader, it is important that you build a foundation of trust at the outset. This is because your team needs to decide what they think of your message before they can decide what they think of you. Once you have established your warmth, your strength is perceived as welcome reassurance of your competence to lead. Connect first and your leadership becomes a gift not a threat.

Team vision boards

If I was going to deliver my vision and achieve my goals, I knew it was important that the team was clear on what that vision was and what goals or objectives we were jointly working towards. To facilitate this, I put up a visual display describing the vision and reaffirming the goals. I also made sure the team vision was copied in all learning documentation. As the team set and started to achieve their goals, the visual display was updated so everyone could see the progress being made.

Vision boards are a great way to capture goals. They visually summarise what someone wants to be, do and have right from the start. Vision boards help a team to dream big and explore the 'what if' scenarios that can arise on the journey towards achieving a goal. Once you know what it is you want to be, do or have you need to take action. This is how you start to make your vision a reality.

When working with the Ignite team, it was important for me that the individual goals the team set fit with the company's goals. I had previously had company goals imposed upon me and I knew what that felt like – and it wasn't very motivating or engaging! This is because when we are forced to take company goals as personal goals, they are not meaningful to us, so it's hard to feel any commitment to them. This is where most leaders fail, because they start out with a goal that their team is not committed to delivering. This means there is little or no willingness from the team to be held accountable for achieving that goal. This is why I gave so much attention to setting team goals that were congruent with the goals of the individuals in the team while simultaneously honouring the goals of the business.

Team goal setting

I started setting goals with the Ignite team within the first two weeks of the programme. Due to only having 12 weeks to work with them, the goal-setting exercise had to start almost immediately. The first activities I got the team to complete were the learning style questionnaires so that I knew how they each learnt best. I then gave them the motivation questionnaire because I needed to know what motivated them. Both of these were important when the team set its goals.

Once the goals where set, they were reviewed daily by the individual team members and then weekly with me during their one-to-one meetings. As time progressed and habits were formed, the amount of time needed for reviewing goals and setting new actions lessened as each team member started to naturally do this for themselves.

Usually, I would have only reviewed goals with each team member on a monthly basis, but as the programme was short and I was addressing employee under-performance, poor attitudes, difficult behaviour and lack of motivation, I needed to review their goals more often. This allowed me to keep every member of the team on track and support them in making the necessary changes to enable them to achieve success.

This was one of the most exciting stages of the Ignite process because I was giving the team some flexibility to be creative with their own goals whilst ensuring they fitted with the overall company goals and vision. I discovered a lot about the team during this period because I had the opportunity to explore with each person what achieving their goals would mean to them. Below is a goal setting story told by one of the Ignite team. I have changed the name of the employees in order to protect their identity and retain confidentiality.

Andy's Story

Andy had worked for the organisation for 10 years and he had been hugely successful. He was earning a substantial salary with regular bonus payments. He had secured a promotion and he continued to take on additional responsibilities.

Andy is a proud man as well as a single father of two daughters. He had been flying high until recently when he had encountered health issues and experienced a change in manager. He was invited to join the Ignite team because he was exhibiting a lack of motivation and was clearly getting bored in his role.

Typically, Andy was someone who struggled to articulate what he wanted to be, do and have so it was important that I adapted my leadership style to suit him. By completing the profiling questionnaires and the values and beliefs elicitations, I established that growth, family and money were important to him. He needed growth to feel a sense of purpose and pride, he wanted to be a role model to his daughters, and he wanted to be recognised as an influential figure in their lives. He would do anything for his family but sometimes this was to the detriment of his own health. Fundamentally, he needed money to put food on the table, pay the bills and enjoy family time such as day trips and holidays, and for buying the girls gifts for their birthdays and Christmas.

When I first started talking to Andy it seemed that money was his driving force, however the reality was very different. It turned out that he loved being 'the expert' – the guy on the pedestal and the one that everyone goes to when they need help. This was a role he enjoyed but it stopped when his new manager was appointed. As a result, he felt "worthless" and "surplus to requirements", which affected his pride, self-esteem and confidence. So, there were all sorts of issues affecting Andy's engagement. I quickly realised that setting a goal aimed at helping him improve his communications with customers would not have floated his boat at all.

Throughout the goal-setting process, Andy and I started to recognise that he needed a goal that was linked to increasing his personal growth. Being in the Ignite team helped him realise that this was a great opportunity to learn new things and build a relationship with a different leader. As a result, the goal he set was not related to 'improving the customer experience' (a company goal) it was about 'inspiring confidence and improving self-esteem in order to display role-model behaviours'. This was how he would be able to grow best and by doing so, naturally improve the customer experience.

It's very easy as leaders to just 'do as we are told'. However as John Adair says, "Management is doing things right, leadership is doing the right things." If you focus on doing the right thing, you will do things right.

SMART Goals

Let's have a look how to set SMART goals that are linked to key motivators, are congruent with core values and that stretch the goal-setter outside of their comfort zone. Go through this process yourself before taking your team through it so you can support and help them with the process from a position of experience.

To create a goal, make sure you always use positive language. Start with: "I want to achieve this goal because…" to get yourself thinking of what is stimulating you to set this goal. Consider what you will gain by achieving this goal. What will be the benefit of achieving it for you, the customers and the business. Make sure you write down your goals and attach actions to them, otherwise they become dreams. Here are some tips on how to create a well-formed goal.

- To be effective, the goal needs to stretch you so you can achieve more than you have before. You also need to make sure that the goal is SPECIFIC, stating exactly what it is you will achieve when you have reached it.
- It needs to have a MEASURE in place. To do this, ask yourself: "How will I measure my success?", "What tangible evidence will I have when I achieve the goal?"
- The goal should be ACHIEVEABLE, which means you have to *believe* this goal can be achieved even though you are going to be stretched outside your comfort zone to achieve something more than you have achieved before.

- The goal should also be REALISTIC. There is no point is setting a goal to achieve something that doesn't fit with your *purpose* (otherwise it may look realistic but you won't be driven to take action, in which case it will never get done). Equally, don't set goals that are unrealistic on a practical level i.e. becoming Wimbledon champion when you're 50 years old, very unfit and have never played tennis before.
- And last but not least, you need to have a deadline so you have a TIMESCALE in which to work to achieve the goal.

SMART is an acronym you have probably heard before. It has been used for a long time and is a recognised system for setting achievable and relevant goals. In order to set a well-formed goal you need to ask the following questions:

S – Is it SPECIFIC?
M – Is it MEASURABLE?
A – Is it ACHIEVEABLE?
R – Is it RELEVANT?
T – Does it have a TIMESCALE?

If the answer to all of these questions is "Yes" then the goal is SMART and it has all the qualities necessary to support the goal-setter in achieving it. If the answer to any of these questions is "no", the goal needs to be revisited so it can be adapted until the answer to all the questions is "yes". This is a fast and effective way to check that a goal is right for you, right now. If you want to make sure a goal has been properly thought-through and considered, ask questions about it. To get you started, here is a list of possible questions you could ask.

- In what way is your goal specific?
- Does it tell you specifically what you are going to do?

- How are you going measure your success?
- What are those measures?
- How achievable is your goal?
- How will you achieve it?
- What is the relevance of the goal?
- How long will it take you to achieve your goal?
- When specifically do you want to achieve your goal?
- What's the ideal timescale for achieving your goal?

These questions will highlight any issues with the goal so it can be amended. A well-formed goal will have a substantial impact on how easily it is achieved by the goal-setter.

The GROW Model

Another great method for setting good goals is the GROW model. It is a simple but effective tool that enables you as a leader and coach to have a conversation with your employee about goal setting. It links into SMART because the first thing you do is explore the goal your team member wants to set. GROW is an acronym for:

G – Goal
R – Reality
O – Options
W – Way forward.

Tips on using GROW

- **Goal**: First of all, set a SMART goal and make sure it is written down.
- **Reality**: Explore the REALITY of the situation. At this moment in time, where is your employee in their development? What evidence do they have that this is true? What is happening on a daily basis that proves this is really happening?

- **Options**: Once your employee has defined their GOAL or 'where they want to be' and the REALITY of the situation they are in, they need to look at all the OPTIONS for getting where they want to go. It is important at this stage that they explore every opportunity. Allow them to brainstorm so they can think without limits: "If there were no barriers, what could I do?" Make sure they get all their ideas out and onto paper.
- **Way forward**: Once they have a long list of possibilities to choose from, you can ask your employee to commit to turning two or three of those opportunities into actions. This becomes the WAY FORWARD and creates an action plan for the achievement of the goal. This means the dream has become a goal with actions attached to it.

To get the process started, ask your team members a series of questions so they can start thinking about what goals they want to set.

Goal

- What do you want to have written down on paper by the end of our session?
- What area of your performance would you like to focus on today?
- What will be the impact on you of achieving this goal?
- What is important to you right now?
- What do you want to achieve?
- When do you want to do it by?
- What do you want instead of the problem?
- On a scale of 1-10 which is the most important issue to you?
- How will you know when you have achieved it?

Reality

- Where are you now in relation to your goal?
- What do you already know to be true about the situation?
- Tell me what is happening at the moment.
- How much control do you have of this situation?
- What is holding you back?
- What have you tried so far?
- What's stopping you from getting what you want?
- What do you need to know that you currently don't know?
- Describe the present situation in more detail.

Options

- What could you do differently?
- What might others do in this situation?
- Is there anyone else you know – or that someone else knows – who has already achieved this?
- What options do you have? What else? (Keep asking this question until they can't think of any more options.)
- What can you do to change the situation?
- How can you affect the outcome?
- What else might you do?
- What else can you bring from your past successes?
- What advice would your best friend give you?

Way Forward

- What are the first steps you need to take?
- What potential obstacles are there?
- How are you going to overcome those obstacles?

- When precisely are you going to take each action step?
- What support do you need, and from whom?
- What is the next step?
- Who needs to know?
- When will you start?
- When will you know you have achieved your goal?
- On a scale of 1-10, how committed are you to taking action?
- On a scale of 1-10, how motivated are you to take action?

These questions will encourage your team to:

- Be ***specific*** about their goal.
- Articulate how they are going to ***measure*** their success.
- Say how they will ***achieve*** their goal.
- Say what the ***relevance*** of their goal is to them.
- Specify over what ***time*** period they are going to deliver it.

Using these questioning methods, it's possible to set a SMART goal that takes someone into their learning zone, is congruent with their core values and satisfies their motivators – all in as little as 30 minutes. It's always good to remind an employee that when they achieve their goal they will also be contributing to the achievement of a bigger organisational goal. Remember to review the goal on a regular basis so if any plans aren't working they can be adapted and any successes can be celebrated.

Book some meetings in your diary and try it out with your team. See for yourself how easy the process is and then invest in a 30 minute session with a coach so you can go through the same process yourself. After all, every coach needs a coach!

Goal-setting tips

Write it down

In order to achieve a goal, it not only needs to be correctly formed, it also needs to be written down. Goals that are not committed to paper are just dreams. Action is required if a goal is going to be achieved – and there is nothing more rewarding than ticking off a list of tasks that lead to reaching a goal (especially if you are motivated by achievement and recognition!). If you write down goals and action lists you are more likely to review your goal on a daily basis and monitor what you are doing to achieve it. I strongly recommend you use visual displays, such as vision boards, to display goals so you know what it is you are doing and why.

Measure progress

In order to review your team's progress towards achieving their goals you need to assess them in your team's one-to-one meetings. To do this, make sure they reflect and prepare before they see you. A quick and easy way of doing this is to ask them to use the following simple review process.

Success

Write down what have you achieved. Remember no matter how small the success, it's still a success. If everyone achieved one per cent more within the team, think how far the team would shift. If you achieved one per cent more towards your goals, think how quickly you'd get there.

Challenges

The challenges you have faced or that you expect to face are probably the result of you working towards your goals so make sure your goals are written down so everyone concerned knows what you are trying to achieve, why you want to achieve it and how you plan to make it happen.

Opportunities

Make sure you keep a written note of all the opportunities that come your way, no matter how absurd or small they may seem to be. Just because you are offered an opportunity, it doesn't mean you are going to accept it. It's important at this stage to document everything because the more information you have, the more choice you have over what you do.

Development

Focus on how you are going to grow and develop both personally and professionally. Make sure you recognise where you currently are in relation to where you want to be so you can see how far you need to go (and how far you have come when you get there!).

Identify the Motivators

Once your team has formed their goals, they need to identify which motivators will be satisfied when they achieve those goals. For example, if money is a key motivator, will the achievement of the goal result in that person earning more money? If it doesn't, the goal may not be motivating enough to inspire action.

As well as checking whether the goal is congruent with the goal-setter's motivators, you also need to check whether it is aligned with an individual's values. You need to do this to make sure the goal is not in conflict with your team member's values. In Andy's case he wanted to become a better role model so he could demonstrate positive attitudes and behaviours, improve his mental health and wellbeing, have a positive impact on his family's lifestyle and improve the customer experience. He believed that achieving this goal would result in him receiving praise which would then raise his confidence, increase his self-esteem and give him the sense that he was adding value – all of which would give him a good feeling about himself and satisfy his kinaesthetic preferences. Ultimately, then his goal was to feel good.

However, this goal was difficult to measure in the usual way. Instead, it needed to be assessed on a daily basis using the mood board. It could also be captured daily in Andy's reflective journal. This way, he was able to identify triggers of positive and negative emotions and the thought patterns that went with them. That made patterns easier to spot and deal with as they became more familiar.

Remove interference

A phrase I like – and that I displayed within the Ignite team area – was from Timothy Gallwey's book: *Inner Game.* In it, he states that: Performance = Potential - Interference (Performance equals Potential minus Interference). This is why it's important to recognise and facilitate the potential in someone. I always look for the good in people and raise their awareness of what they are good at and why, identifying these as their strengths. At the same time, I know it's important to draw their attention to what gets in the way of them achieving greater success; in other words, the interference.

Interference can consist of lots of different things so I asked my team to document all the interference they experience. I started by asking them to identify the interference they experienced within a one-hour time period. I then pushed on and asked them to identify the interference they experienced in a day, in a week and then in a month. Think about what interference you experience. Take a few minutes right now to write down what you notice. What interference do you think the Ignite team experienced in achieving peak performance? What interference do you think got in the way of me achieving peak performance? Below is what I found got in my way:

- Emails.
- My thoughts and feelings.
- The behaviour of others.
- People stopping by for a chat.
- Phone calls.

- Absences.
- Compliance issues.
- Micro managing.
- Dotting the 'I's and crossing the 'T's.
- Meetings.
- Procrastination.

Some of the questions I asked myself so I could get beyond this interference included:

- What is within your circle of control?
- What is within your circle of influence?
- Is what I am currently doing influencing my performance?
- Is what I am doing moving me towards my goal or away from it?

I said to myself: "If you answer these questions, you will learn what you need to change because only you can decide what to change and know what the benefits of that change will be." When I sat down with each of my team I got them to consider how their personal goals aligned with the team's goals, the contact centre's goals and ultimately the organisation's goals.

Move out of the comfort zone

You probably recall me saying that it is important that a goal is motivating if it is going to be achieved. And for a goal to be motivating, it needs to take you out of your comfort zone. If a goal is not challenging enough, how likely are you to achieve that goal? Not very – it'll just seem too boring. Likewise, if a goal is too challenging, what do you think might happen? Again, nothing, because the goal will appear to require too much effort and hard work to even get it started.

The key to success with goal-setting is to make sure that each individual sets a goal that motivates them. That means your job is to check whether the goal stretches them. You need to make sure it stretches them far enough to stimulate them (so they are pushed into their learning zone) and not pushed so far that they go into their panic zone. This is why you need to raise your employee's awareness of which of their motivators the goal is linked to. Motivators predominantly fall into these categories:

- Independence/Freedom
- Recognition
- Achievement
- Leisure Time
- Power
- Prestige
- Money
- Pressure
- Self-Esteem
- Family/Social Life
- Security
- Personal Growth

Ask your team which of their needs they are seeking to fulfil by setting this goal. Is it a financial need? A family need? One that will give them more freedom? Do they need to feel more pressure because this is when they perform at their best? Or do they want to feel more relaxed so they can achieve more?

Next, you need to identify how congruent the goal is with their values. For example, if they value security, will achieving this goal help to secure their future? Remember, the word used to identify a value can differ from person to person so you need to be sure you understand what the word or value means to your team member before you can do this work.

Organisational goals

All organisations have a company vision, which is often expressed in the form of a mission statement. This enables the vision to get filtered down through the organisation so everyone is familiar with it. Everyone then understands that the decisions, projects and initiatives undertaken by the company are in pursuit of the overall company vision.

In my role as the leader of the Ignite team, I had been tasked with the goal of increasing employee engagement by using my coaching skills as well as my other personal qualities. I understood that my goal for the Ignite team was closely linked with the organisation's broader goal of achieving an employee engagement score of 80 per cent in the viewpoint survey, meaning that, ideally, every employee would be at least 80 per cent engaged in the business.

One of the reasons why the business set this target was because it had a bigger goal of becoming number one for financial services. But why would having engaged employees lead to business success? Well, probability states that if you have engaged employees who feel empowered, they will be happy, and if they are happy they will ooze positivity and this will filter down to others in the team and ultimately to customers. If the customer services team is happy and vibrant, customers are more likely to do business with you than if the team is dull and dreary.

Most organisations create performance agreements that state how they want their employees to behave and what they want them to achieve. That means employees have specific targets to achieve and the company documents how well they achieve those targets. However, for the company to be able to achieve its overall goal, employees need to realise their potential too, and that means identifying what might get in the way of their success.

Developing your leadership goals

If you are to succeed in leading your team members in developing their own goals and vision for success, it is important that you identify your own, both as an individual and as a team leader. To do this, you need to identify your main leadership goals, the behaviour you want to develop to support that goal and a secondary or supporting goal that reinforces or feeds back into the main goal.

My main goal as a leader was to be liked and respected [MAIN LEADERSHIP GOAL], however to achieve this, no matter how challenging and how demanding it was, I knew I had to be true to my authentic self. To be true to my authentic self, I knew I would need to have challenging conversations with my team.

As a result of identifying this core goal, I knew I would need to display both confidence and assertiveness [BEHAVIOURAL GOAL] during potentially difficult and challenging conversations in order to raise an employee's awareness of their negative behaviour and the impact it was having on the team's performance. During these conversations the person on the receiving end may have a variety of thoughts and emotions, one of which might be that they don't like what they are hearing. This then leads to the identification of a supporting core goal, which is to demonstrate effective communication [SECONDARY LEADERSHIP GOAL] that results in a positive outcome for me and my team.

As you can see, in order for me to achieve my main leadership goal (being liked and respected) I was going to have to demonstrate one piece of critical behaviour (confidence and assertiveness) in order to help me in achieving my supporting leadership goal (effective communication). Below is a summary of my core goals as a team leader. I have highlighted the key words in describing my goals.

1. To be **liked and respected [MAIN GOAL]** as a leader by displaying **confidence and assertiveness [BEHAVIOUR]** during challenging conversations with my team.
2. To **communicate effectively [SECONDARY GOAL]** when working with my team.

Next, I asked myself some questions so I could elicit more detail around what my goals meant to me and why. Here are the questions I asked myself:

- What specifically does being liked and respected mean to me?
- What specifically is important to me about being liked and respected?
- What are the benefits to me of being liked and respected?
- How will I know I demonstrate confidence?
- What will others see, feel and hear when I display confidence?
- What will others see, feel and hear when I am being assertive?
- What are the specific benefits to me of feeling confident?
- What happens to my thoughts, feeling and emotions when I think about having challenging conversations?
- What's the worst thing that could happen when I have challenging conversations?
- What's the best thing that could happen when I have challenging conversations?
- What's important to me about improving and influencing my team's performance?
- How will I benefit from improving and influencing my team's performance?

By answering these questions, I gained a deeper awareness of why my goals mattered to me, what my fears were around my goals and how I behave when working towards making my goals a reality. It was a big eye-opener for me and so I encourage you to do the same exercise.

Set your leadership goals

Begin by identifying your own goals and vision of what you want to achieve as a leader of your team. Work out which goals you need to achieve in order to make your vision a reality. Next, answer the questions below so you gain a deeper insight into why these goals are important to you including why they motivate you and how they are congruent with your own values and that of the organisation you work within.

- What is your ultimate goal as a leader and what behaviour do you need to commit to in order to achieve it? Has understanding your leadership goal and core behaviour led you to identify a secondary leadership goal? If so, what is it?
- Look at the words you have used to describe your goal. What do those words mean to you?
- What is important to you about your goal?
- What benefits do you want to enjoy as a result of achieving your goal?
- How will you know when you demonstrate your core behaviour?
- What will others see, feel and hear when you display your core behaviour?
- What will others see, feel and hear when you are demonstrating your core behaviour?
- What are the specific benefits to you of feeling the emotions associated with your core behaviour?
- What happens to your thoughts, feeling and emotions when you think about working towards your secondary leadership goal?
- What's the worst thing that could happen?
- What's the best thing that could happen?
- What's important to you about improving and influencing your team's performance?
- How do you benefit by improving and influencing your team's performance?

By answering these questions you will be establishing what 'gain' you expect from achieving your goal. You can go through this process with your employees around their goals as it will help them to become more engaged.

What keeps you moving towards your goal rather than away from it? Or in the words of Bev James, CEO of The Coaching Academy, "what makes you do it or ditch it?" The goal has to be so important that no matter what happens, you choose to do it. However, it's important to remember that ditching a goal is still action and when you ditch a goal it's either because you have a new and more appropriate goal or because the original goal served little or no purpose.

By now you have a variety of tools, techniques, questions and success stories that you can use to help and support your team in forming a vision that fits with that of the organisation as well as with their own personal goals. With this done, you and your team can move forward and start to achieve the success you desire.

RESOURCES FOR
EMPOWERING EMPLOYEE ENGAGEMENT

Go to **www.accendocoaching.co.uk/bonus**

CHAPTER 6
SUCCESS STORIES

A day without learning is a day wasted –
keep growing and be awesome!
Claire Cahill

It was only at the end of the 12-week Ignite Programme when I was gathering together all the success stories that I realised what an impact the programme had had on the team. It was truly inspiring.

These were all employees who had been stuck in their ways, bored in their roles and firmly rooted in their comfort zone. They were no longer challenged. It was fair to say that some of them didn't particularly want to be in the team but came along for the ride. By the end of the programme, each and every member of the Ignite team had a success story to tell and in this chapter I will share all of those stories with you.

For confidentiality purposes and to protect their identity I have changed their names, however when they read this book they will know exactly who I am talking about. I hope they each have a smile on their face when they read about their successes. I have definitely had a smile on my face writing about them. Before I continue to share their stories, let me take you right back to the beginning of the programme.

All companies have a business plan and part of that plan includes a people plan. The Ignite Programme falls under the people plan section and demonstrates that the company invests in employee engagement. In this situation at least nine employees were disengaged. I was under no illusion that I was part of the plan to support the employee engagement programme. I knew the business would view the Ignite Programme as a success if employees remained in the business and became engaged again or chose to leave because the role was no longer right for them. Playing to my strengths and using all of my coaching skills and tools, I was in a win/win situation. However, the personal challenge I had set myself was to have everyone stay and be empowered for peak performance with their true potential unlocked. Did I achieve that?

Without further ado let's hear the Ignite team's stories and discover what the experience of the Ignite Programme was like for them.

Andy's Story

Before joining the Ignite team, Andy had worked for the organisation for 10 years. He had been hugely successful and had earnt 'Exceeding expectations' bonus ratings on a quarterly basis allowing him to rapidly move to the top of his salary scale. Just before he joined the Ignite team, he had experienced a change of manager and hadn't built a relationship with his new leader. Before this, he had always performed consistently well and exceeded customer expectations. You may be asking yourself why Andy was asked to join the Ignite team and the answer is simply that Andy had his own personal issues that he was battling on a daily basis and sometimes those issues impacted his ability to perform. Andy performs better when he is supported by working relationships built on trust and understanding, so joining the Ignite team offered him a great opportunity to experience this while working with me.

Despite having worked for the same organisation for a long time, Andy and I had never worked together before. However, I quickly discovered that Andy didn't learn by reading, so asking him to read *Who Moved My Cheese* was the worst thing I could have done. What did work well for Andy was the Change Cycle where he was asked to look at a simple diagram and plot his mood on it on a daily basis.

This enabled me to have open and honest conversations with him built on mutual trust.

To get to the root cause of some of Andy's issues, I had to build a relationship with him very quickly so I could get him to trust me. I did this by making myself vulnerable and by sharing my personal experiences with him. Andy seeks praise, recognition and he is motivated to earn money so that he can support his family and give his daughters memories that they can treasure. This is where Andy and I built rapport as we had common ground with our goals for our family; he with his daughters and I with my sons.

At the end of the 12-week programme, Andy asked to remain on my team and subsequently took on additional responsibilities. He also took on a work support role and influenced new staff members by sharing his skills, knowledge and expertise.

What Andy is doing 18 months later

Andy is currently planning his family holiday to Florida and taking some time to reflect on his skills so he can apply for new opportunities inside and outside the organisation. The knowledge and skills he gained while on the Ignite team allowed him to address some of his personal issues allowing him to create structured family time that gives him a better work/life balance.

Karen's Story

Karen was in a real pickle before she joined the Ignite team. She had very little confidence in herself or her ability. She struggled to perform consistently and was really confused about how to move forward. She thought she had tried everything and she wasn't sure what else she could do to improve either her performance or the way she felt about herself. Karen didn't want to just give up and she thought that maybe a different manager, direction, views and help might enable her to move forward so she could start to get somewhere. She quickly started to discover a lot about herself while working on the Ignite Programme. At the end of the 12-week programme this is what Karen had to say about the experience.

"The Ignite Programme has helped me on a daily basis with my confidence. Through increasing my confidence my achievements against my key performance indicators improved. It was something so simple: I just changed my 'can't do' attitude into a 'can do and I will try my best' attitude. As well as a pay rise, I now also receive an increased bonus. Best of all, I now have confidence in myself."

What Karen is doing 18 months later

Karen definitely does have confidence! After 10 years she finally decided to face her fears and follow her dreams. She applied for a new job as a mortgage consultant which involves studying. She has successfully passed her CEMAP exam to become qualified. To achieve this, she had to leave the company, which had been her comfort blanket. As a result of flying from the nest, she has continued to grow and is now recognised as a top performer within another company. She has recognised that her skills are transferable so she has flexibility in her career.

Nick's Story

Nick was complacent, comfortable with processes and knew what needed to be done, however he felt he had become stale. He came in to work, did his job and went home. He didn't feel as if he was fulfilling his potential and on some days he recognised it was because he lacked motivation. Nick likes to come into work and do his own thing. He likes the freedom to 'just get on with it'. At the start of the 12 weeks, Nick thought the Ignite Programme would disrupt his comfortable existence and that he would be constantly analysed. Nick felt that he had no challenges at work so coming into Ignite was worth the risk. After all, he had nothing to lose and he might gain something new to motivate him. Rather than me sharing what worked for Nick, I'll let him tell you in his own words.

"Working with Claire was good. She spotted straight away how I like to work, and adapted to suit my style. In other words, she just let me get on with it while at the same time providing feedback and challenges so I could continue to push myself outside my comfort zone.

"She helped me identify ways in which I could manage my early morning motivation issues which helped inspire me for the rest of the day. Claire said she would listen to a few of my calls from the morning when I get in because we had established this was where my calls weren't at my highest standards. This automatically made me focus and put more energy into my calls in the morning, and as a result, this got me into a good habit for the rest of the day. This is a habit I have since carried forward every morning even when I may not be feeling the most awake.

"I also had the chance to complete some SWOT analysis and self-learning exercises. This allowed me to identify my strengths and weaknesses as well as consider the potential opportunities and threats. By highlighting how I can improve as a person helped me realise that I had potential to do more.

"Since Ignite I have started doing more non-phone work, such as peer-to-peer coaching with new members of staff so I can share best practice. I have attended trial sessions run by managers to test the effectiveness of practices before rolling them out to other consultants e.g. "Effective Questioning" sessions. I then ran these sessions with members of my team afterwards.

"I am currently achieving Exceed bonus ratings. I now feel I have the opportunity to progress and that I am a more valued employee in the company. Prior to Ignite I was meeting customers' needs. Now I feel I am sharing some of my experience and knowledge with other consultants to help them in their role too."

What Nick is doing 18 months later

Nick applied for a role in the branch network and secured a promotion. He is now going to share all of the customer services knowledge he gained in the contact centre in a face-to-face environment, so proving that all his skills are transferable and that he can be an asset in the branch network.

Jack's Story

Before Jack came into the Ignite Programme, he had had a pretty rough time. His manager had been off sick for a while and a temporary manager was standing in. Jack wasn't getting on with the temporary manager's style of coaching at all. He had also been removed from his work support role before he had even done it for a week. He was very disheartened and at an all-time low both personally and professionally. Jack felt that work had got very repetitive as a result of being around the same people for the last few years.

When he joined the team, Jack wondered why he was in it and what he was going to gain from the programme. Once he understood a little more about what was going to happen over the 12 weeks, and realised that he knew some of the people on the team, he felt more at ease. The main reason Jack took the opportunity to join the Ignite team was that he wanted to prove he had lots of potential and that the reason he had previously been given opportunities was not just because he did well in an interview. He knew that if the Ignite concept was successful, he would probably be considered for new opportunities.

Jack found that just being on the team improved his relationships with more experienced members of staff in the contact centre. Jack learnt lots of new techniques through the coaching challenges and was able to experience a variety of approaches to managing different kinds of customer and life situations. Jack enjoyed the reflection exercises where he had to assess himself so he could discover the type of person he is and the type of person he wants to be. He was able to focus on becoming an emotionally stronger and more agile individual.

Jack found it helpful to complete the SWOT analysis and asked his manager to complete it too so that he could compare what he believed about his situation with what others saw. By doing this he was able to understand what his strengths and weaknesses were and what opportunities he could develop. He used this for his goal-setting exercise. This is what Jack had to say about his experience in Ignite

"I've not seen any financial impact of team Ignite personally, however at the time I didn't have any financial motivation because I was going through a very difficult situation and so I just wanted some stability and normality to help me through a rough time.

"Team Ignite helped me to get back on my feet and it re-energised me as a person so I could look at situations in a whole new light compared to how I used to do it. Personally, I feel more confident and motivated both in and outside work. Others have noticed this too.

"At work it has helped me to deliver a higher level of customer service and my energy has increased around my team as a result. I now want to do more things around the team. I'm hoping to use everything that I learnt during my time on ignite with the new starters that I have been chosen to mentor.

"I hope to use my newly-found confidence to deliver presentations, give feedback and praise and also help mould new staff into working in the organisation's unique way. I'm really looking forward to the new challenges."

What Jack is doing 18 months later?

Jack continues to display his confidence and has since decided to pursue a career with another company so he can more easily play to his strengths. He still works in financial services and is taking his learning to a new level.

Lisa's Story

Before joining Ignite, Lisa was tired. She was working a lot of hours because she was doing overtime so her work/life balance was unhealthy. During this time, her customer service experience had been affected in a negative way and her focus was on personal issues. Lisa was demotivated and stressed. Her driving goal was money. Lisa had no reservations about joining Ignite and was looking forward to the opportunity for change.

Lisa had worked for the company for nearly two years but she never had a smile on her face when she came to work. Her manager frequently cancelled their one-to-one meetings so it was only when she was told her bonus rating that Lisa got any feedback on her performance. She was stressed and appeared disruptive to others.

She was brought into the Ignite team so that I could support the existing team manager by coaching her around her behaviour and draw her attention to the impact this behaviour was having on those around her. During the first two weeks she was in and out of my office all the time as I addressed the behaviour I was experiencing.

Using my coaching skills, I gradually started to explore her beliefs and the impact it was having on her at work and in her daily life. I did this by asking open questions, challenging her beliefs and probing her to look deeper. I also got completely comfortable with silences. I listened and I didn't judge. As her beliefs started to unfold, I realised that Lisa had been holding on to negative thoughts and feelings for years. There were things that had happened in her past but were still affecting her years later.

Lisa was definitely unhappy and well outside her comfort zone but unhappily outside her comfort zone because her mood could get no lower. Lisa was in the 'depression stage' of change and she didn't like it. This was a great opportunity for her to make a choice. She could choose to stay where she was and be unhappy or she could choose to change.

Thankfully she decided to change. Rather than viewing the world as a negative place, she decided to see positive benefits around every corner. Before long she was achieving goals she had set herself and her performance was improving. At last, Lisa was coming to work with a smile on her face and it wasn't long before she was asking to take on additional responsibilities and actively looking for opportunities to shine.

At the end of the 12-week programme she had enjoyed herself so much that she requested a permanent transfer to my team. Lisa realised that she needed structure in her day and by having regular one-to-one meetings, coaching sessions and development time, she felt empowered to step up to the mark. She knew her performance was going to be challenged but also that her contribution was valued. For the first time in a long time, all of her motivators were being met. She felt secure, she was being recognised for her achievements and she was earning a bonus.

Lisa continued to grow and develop after the completion of the Ignite Programme and within 6 months she had secured her first promotion to the position of senior consultant, through which she also took on supervisory responsibilities.

What Lisa is doing 18 months later

Lisa is still coming to work with a smile on her face and she is now recognised as a top performer across the whole contact centre. She has taken on a complaint-handling role as part of a pilot scheme and she is leading the way with her organisational skills. She consistently articulates how she adds value to the business across her own team and the site. She is recognised as a role model and a natural successor to a leadership role. She has had a truly remarkable journey, one of which she is extremely proud. Lisa's thoughts about the Ignite Programme are below.

"Working with Claire was a completely different experience to how I had been managed before and she met my personal preferences and gave me the structure I needed. Since then I have incorporated this into my life and feel that I am more structured both at work and at home. She also helped me identify triggers which cause negative behaviours and put into place coping methods.

"I can't pick just one financial benefit I got from the programme, but the two best are achieving an Exceed bonus rating on more than one occasion and being promoted to the position of Senior Consultant, something I never thought I would have the patience to deliver against on a daily basis. I now consistently have a positive attitude to both work and home life. Since working with Claire I feel more comfortable and confident at work and within my role. This has subsequently spilled over into my personal life. I truly think that without Ignite I would have either gone off sick with work related stress or I would have left the company."

Lucy's Story

When she joined the Ignite team, Lucy had no motivation whatsoever. She was underperforming and had no sense of direction. She realised that there were opportunities, but they always seemed to be filled by the same people every time. The Ignite Programme enabled her to spend time away from her team. The opportunity moved her out of her comfort zone and gave her the chance to stand out from the crowd.

Lucy felt scared about being away from her team. She was lively and often increased the energy and morale when she was there. She had just started getting involved with her colleagues and was beginning to enjoy being at work so she didn't want to be away from the people with whom she was most comfortable.

Lucy thought she had been placed on the Ignite team as a last ditch attempt to get her where she needed to be before starting performance management procedures. It's fair to say she was very apprehensive. Lucy decided to share her thoughts and feelings with her manager and this conversation showed her that the situation wasn't as bad as she imagined. In fact, the Ignite programme was an opportunity for her to shine. This new perspective allowed her to embrace the challenge.

It wasn't long before Lucy realised being on the Ignite team was great because she got to spend her days with a new group of friendly people she enjoyed working with. She found there was no awkwardness because all the consultants were well-established despite being from different teams. Through the team-building exercises, the team got to know each other on a new level and she soon discovered that they were all genuinely interested in each other. This is what Lucy had to say about her experience at the end of the programme.

"I was coached and managed very differently and it gave me an insight as to why Claire was so successful with her own team. The experience inspired me to do well and I wanted to be in a position to coach people, too. Since Ignite I have consistently delivered in my role and this has been recognised through bonus and appraisal ratings. I was also promoted to a Senior Consultant Supervisor role which resulted in an increased salary.

"I have managed to secure a place on the next Team Manager Development Programme, which has helped to inspire my confidence and boost my self-esteem. What I find I do more now is to set myself goals to achieve because it gives me something to focus on. I then make sure I celebrate my successes when I achieve my goals."

What Lucy is doing 18 months later

Lucy is still setting goals, achieving them and celebrating success. She has covered for teams in their manager's absence and has also supported new starters in a work support role.

Daniel's Story

Daniel had worked for the organisation for about three years. He had good working relationships with his team and managers across the site. He had been promoted quite rapidly within this time including covering for team managers on the Team Manager Development Programme. Recently, he had applied for a permanent team manager role but had been unsuccessful. This had impacted his confidence and self-esteem. As a result, his pride had been dented and he felt very under-valued.

Daniel was on my team and I had nominated him so being on the Ignite team was a test of his emotional resilience. He was holding on to a lot of anger and this was fuelling his negative behaviour. I decided to recommend that he joined the Ignite team. When he discovered this, Daniel was very confused. Why was he joining this team? After all, wasn't this the team for under-performers, those with a bad attitude or who clearly didn't want to be there?

Although Daniel didn't realise it, there was method in my madness but first I needed to convince him that this was the best move for him. I made him aware that he would be working alongside experienced employees and this should free him from having to constantly answer questions from his existing team allowing him time for his own personal development.

Daniel reluctantly joined the team but within days found himself enjoying the whole experience. I heard him laughing and joking with the team. When I asked him how he was feeling he said, "I haven't worked with these people for such a long time and it's really good to be around them again." He acknowledged that it was nice not to have questions fired at him constantly and that it was good to have adult conversations with like-minded people.

It wasn't long before I saw Daniel's competitive edge start to come to the surface. I had always known that competition was one of Daniel's motivators and now I saw it in action. He was soon seeking recognition for being the top performer in the team. Daniel started to demonstrate his natural leadership capabilities by sharing tips with the team and making sure everyone was equipped to deal with their own personal challenges.

Daniel responded to all the challenges that were set and he completed all the learning and development tools. By reading the book *Who Moved My cheese?* when he came into the Ignite Programme, Daniel was able to identify the character with whom he was most closely aligned – though he was a different character when he left!

At the end of the Ignite Programme Daniel knew what his strengths were as well as his weaknesses and he had started to explore many opportunities available to him. He decided that if he couldn't secure a team manager opportunity within the organisation he would secure one outside! He did just that but because he was engaged within the organisation he decided not to take the manager opportunity. He has stayed with the business, and I was delighted because I knew he would one day secure a management position within the company.

What Daniel is doing 18 months later

Since the end of the 12-week programme, Daniel has secured a permanent Team Manager's role within the organisation. I even had the pleasure of working alongside him for over a year. He has a high-performing team and continues to grow within his role. He uses all he learnt from his Ignite experience within his existing team and continues to go from strength to strength.

Tim's Story

Before joining the Ignite team, Tim had been in his role for the previous eight years so it's fair to say he was comfortable in it. Although he took on additional responsibilities to support his manager, he definitely wasn't being stretched. What Tim wanted to get out of his time on the Ignite Programme was some clarity about his future and his goals. He identified what motivated him and where his strengths lay. He discovered he just wanted a simple uncomplicated life. He is happy to come to work, do a good job and go home. He loves to travel and spend quality time with his wife. Tim got the most benefit out of the personality profiling because he realised 'this is who I am and I'm okay with that'.

What he found by being in the Ignite team was that he doesn't necessarily want additional responsibility and that he enjoyed being around other experienced consultants. Every team needs someone like Tim, someone they can rely on to do a good job. Tim realised that he had a good work/life balance and that this was his main reason for remaining in his role. This was the clarity he wanted and he was both happy with what he discovered and comfortable articulating it.

What Tim is doing 18 months later

Tim has moved teams and is now working for Daniel. Due to Tim and Daniel working together in Ignite, Daniel knows how to play to Tim's strengths so suddenly Tim is thriving in his role. He still has his work/life balance and enjoys travelling the world with his wife.

Aaron's Story

Aaron was bored. He had been in his role for eight years and he felt he wasn't getting anywhere very fast. His performance was suffering because he was bored and because he could be easily distracted by chat about irrelevant facts, just to pass the time of day. It was important that I raised Aaron's awareness of his habits sooner rather than later. I shared information about both the comfort zone and the change curve with him, and asked him to plot where he was on the curve. I used this tool on a weekly basis to help him identify his progress. Aaron found the SWOT analysis very useful because it highlighted opportunities that he could take advantage of and that played to his strengths. It also helped him to develop skills that could further support him in his role.

When I set goals with Aaron, I knew it was important that they stretched him. They needed to take him outside his comfort zone where he could satisfy his motivators: growth and recognition. Once his goals had been linked to his motivators and values, he was able to push himself outside his comfort zone and develop rapidly.

At the end of the programme, Aaron had secured an opportunity to support new staff in the business and as a result he soon started to share his skills and knowledge. Like Lucy, he also applied for the Team Manager Development Programme and secured a place. This resulted in him managing the team he had left to join Ignite, which he did successfully for at least six months. When the opportunity came up for a permanent position he didn't secure the role, however he demonstrated his emotional resilience and asked for interview feedback. He then implemented a development plan so he could secure a position in the future.

What Aaron is doing 18 months later

Aaron implemented his Team Manager Development plan and has since secured a permanent leadership role with another company. The new role is giving Aaron a valuable opportunity to use his skills and gain a management qualification, something he may not have done if he'd stayed with the business.

My Success Story

What more can I say? I was blown away by the whole experience of leading the Ignite team. I hope you can see from the stories I have shared that the power of coaching has clearly been demonstrated as it was a key factor in the success of the team and the individuals on it. I am passionate about the transformational power of coaching for all concerned and now hope you are too.

As a coach there is nothing more powerful than having an employee stand on their own two feet and clearly articulate their thoughts, feelings and experiences in the knowledge that they have made the choice to change and have chosen to be happy, positive and motivated. As a leader, there is nothing more empowering that seeing, feeling and hearing your team set challenges, step outside their comfort zone, grow as individuals and then celebrate success.

What I am doing 18 months later

I'm still using coaching techniques with teams I manage and reaping the rewards and recognition through the team's achievements. I have recently taken on a six-month secondment as an operations manager in a contact centre fulfilling my dream of working with leaders, implementing the tools and techniques described in this book and encouraging the managers I am working with to be their brilliant best as leaders and coaches on a daily basis. I am continuing to grow as a coach and leader investing in my own continued personal development. I am employing a coach to support me with the writing and production of this book and I am also working towards my level 5 Leadership and Management qualification with the Chartered Management Institution.

"Dream, Believe, Achieve –
Unlock your true potential and make it happen."

RESOURCES FOR EMPOWERING EMPLOYEE ENGAGEMENT

Go to **www.accendocoaching.co.uk/bonus**

CHAPTER 7
NEXT STEPS

What options are now available? How can you implement the 12-Week Ignite Programme? You can follow this process with your existing teams using the book as a tool to guide you. Make sure you are clear about what you are doing and why. If you decide to use this approach but you don't already have a coach or a mentor working with you then I strongly recommend that you get one. Every coach needs a coach! I have one myself. I hope you will agree from the success stories that the concept works so I hope you feel inspired to try it out.

Top Tips

Always play to your strengths

If you know you are a great coach and leader then use this to your advantage, likewise if you know that this is an area that you need to develop then seek out a great coach, leader or mentor and ask them to help you develop your skills. Identify people in your team who have the skills you need and use them in your team. Remember, together, everyone achieves more.

Individuals and teams respond differently to change at work, however change needs to be managed effectively. In this book, I have only scraped the surface of what there is to know about change. I have shared some of my best reads on change, however there will be lots more books and resources out there that can support you on your journey. From my experience, when organisations go through big change programmes, it's vitally important that you and your team both feel engaged with the process.

Failure to engage effectively will lead to a lack of empowerment and will ultimately affect performance.

Do you want the best people to leave? I recently read an article by David W Richard about why good employees leave a company. Basically, he says the reason a business loses good people is due to management. More than any other single reason given, the reason good employees either stay and thrive in an organisation or leave it (taking their knowledge, experience and contacts straight to the competition) is their immediate manager. "People leave managers not companies" write the authors Marcus Buckingham and Curt Coffman. "So much money has been thrown at the challenge of keeping good people – in the form of better pay, better perks and better training – when, in the end, turnover is mostly a manager issue." If you have a turnover problem, look first to your managers and supervisors.

An employee's primary need often has less to do with money than with how he or she is treated by the business and whether he or she feels valued. Much of this depends on the immediate manager. As John Drucker says, "Management is doing things right; leadership is doing the right things." Why not choose to be the leader who does the right thing and does it right?

Don't be afraid to ask

No matter who you are, whether you are a CEO, the director of your own company, a leader or an employee, it's okay to be vulnerable and to ask for help. Not only will you grow as an individual, others around you will see that you are human after all. Do you really want to be superman or superwoman? Why not just be your brilliant best every day? After all you are unique.

Continuously Challenge

Upwards, downwards, sideways, look in the mirror and ask yourself what you need to change. If you always do what you've always done, you'll always get the same result so challenge yourself. Be innovative. To keep people engaged you need to do something different, otherwise it becomes boring and then you know what happens, comfort sets in. Be courageous and dare to be different.

Invest in your people

If necessary bring in experts; coaching is an investment in your people and if you invest in your people, you will reap the rewards many times over.

RESOURCES FOR EMPOWERING EMPLOYEE ENGAGEMENT

Go to **www.accendocoaching.co.uk/bonus**

RESOURCES

Tools

Team formation

You can learn more about the Storming, Forming, Norming and Performing stages of team development at: www.mindtools.com.

Personality Profiling: DISC

If you want to know your own DISC personality profile as well as that of your team members please contact me via my website www.accendocoaching.co.uk to arrange a coaching session.

Fisher's Personal Transition Curve

Fisher's Personal Transition Curve is a free resource that you can get from www.businessballs.com. You can also read the theory behind the Personal Transition Curve and explanations about how it works by visiting Business Balls: www.businessballs.com/personalchangeprocess.htm.

VAK questionnaire

Go to www.businessballs.com to download the VAK questionnaire and complete it for free.

Defining motivational language

There is a questionnaire you can complete that will help you identify the meaning of a person's motivational words. It is available online and from my website as a free download at www.accendocoaching.co.uk.

Books

There are many books that discuss the change curve and the transitions people go through during a period of change or growth. Below is a list of books you might like to read if you would like to learn more.

Who Moved My Cheese? – Dr Spencer Johnson
Our Iceberg is Melting – John Kotter
My Fire's Gone Out – Liam O'Connell
rEvolution: How to thrive in crazy times – Bill Lucas
Transitions: Making sense of life's changes – William Bridges
Feel the Fear and Do It Anyway – Dr Susan Jeffers

RESOURCES FOR EMPOWERING EMPLOYEE ENGAGEMENT

Go to **www.accendocoaching.co.uk/bonus**

1. Team fact sheet
2. Maslow's Hierarchy of Needs
3. Karpman Drama Triangle
4. Comfort Zone
5. 8 Steps to Successful Change
6. Beliefs Checklist
7. 4 Stages of Team Development

ABOUT CLAIRE CAHILL AND ACCENDO COACHING

I founded Accendo Coaching and Training in 2012 after qualifying with Distinction as a Personal Performance Coach through The Coaching Academy. I subsequently continued with my studies with The Coaching Academy and again qualified with Distinction as a Corporate and Executive coach.

I never stop learning because I never want to stop growing. Through investing in my continued personal development I became a qualified DISC consultant with the guidance of Bev James, CEO of The Coaching Academy. Since then, I have followed Bev James's approach of "do it or ditch it" and have written this book.

I am also a qualified EFT (Emotional Freedom Technique) practitioner and can use tapping to work on the emotional baggage that people carry around with them. I am a registered practitioner with the AAMET and I am governed by their ethics and conduct guidelines.

I would be delighted to support you and your team on your journey of self-discovery. Please contact me if you would like further information about any of my services.

- Website: www.accendocoaching.co.uk
- Email: claire@accendocoaching.co.uk
- Facebook – Accendo Coaching & Training
- Linked In – Claire Cahill
- Twitter – @CahillClaire

I look forward to hearing from you. Until then start implementing the ideas in this book so you can Ignite Your Team for Peak Performance and unlock your own and your team's true potential.